# S
# AND STONES
# and Other Student Essays

FIFTH EDITION

EDITED BY
LAWRENCE BARKLEY
*MT. SAN JACINTO COLLEGE, MENIFEE VALLEY*

RISE B. AXELROD
*UNIVERSITY OF CALIFORNIA, RIVERSIDE*

CHARLES R. COOPER
*UNIVERSITY OF CALIFORNIA, SAN DIEGO*

BEDFORD / ST. MARTIN'S
Boston • New York

**For Bedford/St. Martin's**

*Developmental Editor:* Gregory S. Johnson
*Production Editor:* Maria Teresa Burwell
*Senior Production Supervisor:* Dennis J. Conroy
*Art Director:* Lucy Krikorian
*Text Design:* Paul Agresti
*Copy Editor:* Alice Vigliani
*Cover Design:* Lucy Krikorian
*Composition:* Macmillan India Limited
*Printing and Binding:* Haddon Craftsmen

*President:* Joan E. Feinberg
*Editorial Director:* Denise B. Wydra
*Editor in Chief:* Nancy Perry
*Director of Marketing:* Karen R. Melton Soeltz
*Director of Editing, Design, and Production:* Marcia Cohen
*Managing Editor:* Erica T. Appel

Library of Congress Control Number: 2003107542



Manufactured in the United States of America.

9 8 7 6 5 4
f e d c b a

*For information, write:* Bedford/St. Martin's, 75 Arlington Street, Boston, MA 02116 (617-399-4000)

ISBN: 0-312-40738-6

# *Preface*

In its fifth edition, *Sticks and Stones and Other Student Essays* continues the honorable tradition of its predecessors: to celebrate student writing. The first edition, *The Great American Bologna Festival,* was published in 1991 in response to the overwhelmingly positive reaction to the student essays featured in the Instructor's Resource Manual for the second edition of *The St. Martin's Guide to Writing.* Choosing representative essays for this new *Sticks and Stones* has been no easier a task than it was for the previous editions, for we had the opportunity to read a great deal of good student writing that excited our appreciation and respect. Although at times the undertaking seemed daunting, we relished the experience of discovering the voices contained in new submissions—as well as revisiting those of past submissions.

## An Overview of *Sticks and Stones and Other Student Essays*

*Sticks and Stones* is a reader designed to accompany *The St. Martin's Guide to Writing.* Its organization mirrors Part I of *The Guide,* and each chapter introduces student-written essays that model the principles described in *The Guide.* Taken together, the essays in *Sticks and Stones* and *The Guide* offer students a wonderfully diverse range of subjects and voices to explore and consider.

Chapter 1, an introductory chapter, uses examples from the essays in later chapters of *Sticks and Stones* to suggest ways the essays may be of use in enhancing the reader's own writing. Chapters 2 to 10 feature 36 student-written essays in nine different genres, from "Remembering Events" to "Arguing a Position" to "Interpreting Stories," and each of these chapters begins with an introduction to the genre and commentary on its essays. Also included are two final sections: "A Note on the Copyediting," which explains the important role of editing in improving student writing, and "Sample Copyediting," which features a sample draft with hand-edits of Erick Young's essay "Only She" so that students can see the editing process in black and white.

## New to the Fifth Edition

With the helpful guidance of the many instructors who reviewed the fourth edition, we have made several exciting changes in this new edition.

***New Essays.*** In addition to the 25 most popular essays from the fourth edition, we have included 11 new and engaging pieces—nearly a third of the collection: Amber Sky Emanuel's "Limitless Hope" (Remembering Events), Angel Nguyen's "The Eyes in the Mirror" (Remembering People), Brenda Crow's "The Dance with Glass" (Writing Profiles), Glenda Sourisseau's "Homemade Horror" (Writing Profiles), Thomas Beckfield's "Banning Cell Phone Use While Driving" (Arguing a Position), Jeff Varley's "High School Starting Time" (Proposing a Solution), Heather Parker's "Electronic Medical Records and Privacy Issues" (Proposing a Solution), Jacqueline Newton and Cynthia Reinhard's "Sea Sick" (Proposing a Solution), James Rollins's "The Little Film That Could . . . and Did" (Justifying an Evaluation), Robert Nava's "May I Have This Dance?" (Justifying an Evaluation), and Krista Gonnerman's "Pharmaceutical Advertising" (Speculating about Causes).

***Descriptive Table of Contents.*** We have redesigned the table of contents so that each essay's entry features a descriptive "essence" quote that gives the reader a quick preview of that essay.

***Essays with Visual Elements.*** Two new essays—Jacqueline Newton and Cynthia Reinhard's co-authored "Sea Sick" (Proposing a Solution) and Robert Nava's "May I Have This Dance?" (Justifying an Evaluation)—model how students can effectively incorporate visual elements into their writing.

***2003 MLA Documentation.*** Each of the documented essays in the fifth edition conforms to the 2003 MLA guidelines for citing sources, including Internet sources, so that students have up-to-date models for their own source-based writing.

***Online Essay Submissions.*** To make the essay submission process quicker and easier, students and instructors can now submit essays to us online at *The Guide*'s companion Web site: <bedfordstmartins.com/theguide>. Students and instructors can also submit essays to us by regular mail, using the forms on pp. 193–194.

## Suggestions for Using *Sticks and Stones and Other Student Essays*

*Sticks and Stones* is an ancillary that can be used in tandem with *The St. Martin's Guide to Writing*. You could ask students to read a chapter in *Sticks and Stones*, select their favorite essay, and analyze how it meets the requirements—as outlined in *The Guide*—of its genre. Helpful starting points for such an exercise are the "Analyzing Writing Strategies" and "Summary of Basic Features" sections in Chapters 2 to 10 of *The Guide*. You might want to assign groups of students individual essays within each chapter of *Sticks and Stones*, inviting each group to discuss how the essay addresses the assignment in *The Guide* that it is meant to fulfill. Because the essays in *Sticks and Stones* are so diverse, you and your students could explore essays that model many different ways of organizing ideas, structuring sentences, using vocabulary and tone, and addressing audience and genre. To inspire thoughtful revision and editing, you could have your students submit essays that were based on assignments in *The Guide*—or even inspired by essays in *Sticks and Stones* itself—for publication consideration in the campus newspaper or the next editions of *The Guide* and *Sticks and Stones*. These suggestions are but a few of the numerous uses for *Sticks and Stones*, and we would be delighted to learn how *you* use this book, as well as what you would like to see in the next edition.

## Acknowledgments

We are grateful to many people who made this edition of *Sticks and Stones* a reality. Most of all, we would like to thank the hundreds of students who have conceived, drafted, written, revised, and polished the essays we have received over the years. Although we can't include every essay submitted to us, we have read each one with interest, enjoyment, and care.

We also send countless thanks to the instructors who encouraged their students to submit their work for this collection or who submitted their students' work themselves. *Sticks and Stones* would not exist without the efforts of these instructors, and for their kindness, generosity, and participation, we are truly grateful.

Many thanks go to the instructors whose students' work is published in this fifth edition for the first time: Alpha Anderson-Delap, Front Range Community College, Larimer; Lawrence Barkley, Mt. San Jacinto College, Menifee Valley; Kristin Brunnemer, Mt. San Jacinto College, Menifee Valley; Patricia Carlson, Rose-Hulman Institute of Technology; Joshua Fenton, University of California, Riverside; Denise Henson, South Piedmont Community College; Jennifer Jacobo, Mt. San Jacinto College, Menifee Valley; Cindy Okamura, Riverside Community College; Cristal Renzo, Elizabethtown College; and Joanna Tardoni, Western Wyoming Community College.

Many thanks also go to the following instructors, whose insightful reviews of the fourth edition helped to shape the fifth: Susan Bailor, Front Range Community College; Kristi Brock, Northern Kentucky University; Emerson Case, Marshall University; Gary Christenson, Elgin Community College; Chitralekha Duttagupta, Arizona State University; Kristi Eiler, Northern Kentucky University; Daniel Gonzalez, Louisiana State University; Heather M. Hoyt, Arizona State University; Arden Jansen, Gulf Coast Community College; Robyn McGee, Longview Community College; Michael Montgomery, Life University; Keith Reierstad, Aims Community College; Robert E. Rubin, Wright State University; Michaela Safadi, Arizona State University; Rachelle Smith, Emporia State University; Jennifer Sorensen, Western Wyoming Community College; Scott R. Stankey, Anoka-Ramsey Community College; Kate Wilson, The Catholic University of America; and Mari H. York, Northern Kentucky University.

We would also like to extend our sincere appreciation to Greg Johnson of Bedford/St. Martin's for his thoughtful guidance, his invaluable editorial suggestions, and the considerable energy and enthusiasm that he brought to this project. And, of course, we thank Elizabeth Rankin and Paul Sladky, whose fine work on previous editions of this book set the standards for everything that followed.

Lawrence Barkley
Rise B. Axelrod
Charles R. Cooper

# Contents

# *To the Student* 1

The essays in *Sticks and Stones and Other Student Essays* were written by students like you in writing classes like yours across the country. You will find that the writers whose work is collected here are as sincere in their purpose as individuals who write professionally. Their writing is committed and energetic, and they are determined to seize their readers and provoke a response. The tone of their writing is not, "Gee, would you *mind* reading my work?" nor is it that of a class assignment written for an audience of one—the instructor. Instead, these essays clearly belong to writers who believe in what they say, who are writing for an audience they know exists beyond themselves and those grading their work.

You might be thinking, "I'm not like the students whose essays appear in this book; I could never write that well . . . or even get my writing published." To become good at something, whether dribbling a basketball, playing the piano, sewing a quilt, or balancing a chemical equation, you must practice. Writing is no different. To become a good writer you must read, analyze, and, *of course*, write. When you become focused, when you are given the opportunity to write and share your work with others, a metamorphosis will begin. You will no longer think of yourself as someone who is merely completing an assignment for your writing class; you will begin to think of yourself as a writer, as someone with something worth saying.

The essays in this collection can help you with your own writing by giving you ideas for topics. If you are writing a remembered-event essay, you might try thinking of a time when you made an important discovery about life or yourself. Amber Sky Emanuel, author of "Limitless Hope," selects as her topic an incident that marked an emotional awareness of others' ability to survive when survival itself seemed impossible. Should your instructor ask you to write about a remembered person, you may quickly discover that although a number of individuals have influenced your life, there is one whom you remember vividly or one about whom you have unresolved feelings or ideas you would like to explore. The authors of the essays in Chapter 3, "Remembering People," have all identified individuals who have had profound effects on their lives. If you are assigned a profile essay, exploring a person or place may lead you to unexpected discoveries. Sarah Sucher, in "No Nuns Here," profiles a midwife and learns that her own ideas of the profession are far from accurate. An investigation into why an individual or a group acted in a way you considered outrageous or extraordinary can lead to an essay in which you speculate about causes. Reese Mason's "Basketball and the Urban Poor" examines why a young man would risk his life to play what many consider nothing more than a game.

The essays here may also help you find solutions to problems in your own writing. Are you trying to convey a mood? To help readers understand the anxiety of leaving home for the first time, Scott Weckerly, author of "Free Falling," concludes his remembered-event essay with a metaphor to express how he feels. Are you wondering how to describe a professional activity? Brenda Crow's "The Dance with Glass" stylistically reveals how an individual is able to blend the necessities of a trade with a passion for an art. Are you seeking an incisive way to present one side of a difficult issue? To express the zealous opposition voiced by those against the reintroduction of wolves into Yellowstone, Keely Cutts, in her arguing-a-position essay, "Wolves in Yellowstone," quotes individuals directly rather than merely telling us of their opposition to reintroducing the canines. Are you looking for a technique to orient your audience? Robert Nava uses visuals as points of reference for readers of his justifying-an-evaluation essay, "May I Have This Dance?" There are numerous other strategies the authors in *Sticks and Stones* have used, techniques with which you will become familiar as you read and analyze their essays.

These essays also provide concrete examples of how other students have used different writing strategies to present their subjects. For example, Ilene Wolf favorably *compares* the magazine *Buzzworm* to other environmental magazines in her evaluative "*Buzzworm*: The Superior Magazine." In his remembered-event essay, "The Relationship," Curtis Dean Adams creates a *dominant impression* in the description of his father. In her proposing-a-solution essay, "Electronic Medical Records and Privacy Issues," Heather Parker facilitates her readers' moving easily from one paragraph to the next by using *transitions* that appropriately and logically link her ideas. And Glenda Sourisseau, in her profile essay, "Homemade Horror," introduces her subject with a vivid *anecdote.*

Additionally, the essays illustrate that research may be conducted in both traditional and alternative venues. To provide supporting evidence for their points, the authors have conducted personal interviews; consulted books, magazine and newspaper articles, institutional reports, and electronic databases; watched both films and television programs; surfed the Internet; and visited art galleries. Depending on your subject and genre, you could also conduct an observation, distribute surveys, or cite a musical composition, live performance, speech, or even a map. Sources are as varied as subjects, and you should not feel compelled or obligated to limit your research to the library.

As you read a particular essay in *Sticks and Stones,* we encourage you to refer to the "Analyzing Writing Strategies" and "Summary of Basic Features" sections in Chapters 2 to 10 of *The St. Martin's Guide to Writing.* These activities will help you better understand each genre and its characteristics. Knowing the attributes of a genre will enable you to compose in that genre more confidently.

Last, thinking in terms of writing for publication will help you establish a clearer focus, purpose, and sense of audience. As you develop your essay, ask yourself, "What would the readers of *Sticks and Stones* need to know in order to understand me?" Remember: even though writing for publication may seem a daunting task, with few exceptions all published writings, including the essays in this collection, started out as *rough drafts.*

*Sticks and Stones* would not exist without the creativity of real students—real *writers*—like you. Put yourself in it! We invite you to submit your writing to us for publication consideration in the next edition of this collection. We also invite instructors to encourage their students to submit their work for this collection or to submit the best of their students' work themselves. You will find a submission form on pp. 193–94; you may also submit papers online at <bedfordstmartins.com/theguide>.

# 2 *Remembering Events*

Writers look to their immediate or distant pasts to choose an event to write about. Regardless of proximity, however, the techniques for telling a story don't change: first, the narrative should be interesting, entertaining, and memorable; second, the presentation of the people and places that inhabit the story should be vividly presented; and third, the autobiographical significance of the event should be clear. The essays in this chapter focus on events from adult life as well as the more distant events of childhood. All, however, create resonant, dramatic scenes in which readers can easily insert themselves.

The opening lines of Nicole Ball's "Sticks and Stones" prepare readers to face the one person from childhood remembered with contempt, trepidation, and dread: the bully. Although Ball conveys her experiences in a temporally linear style, the suspense builds toward a climax as the bully becomes more and more aggressive. The day comes when the bully finally goes too far, and readers see a resolution to the childhood chant, "Sticks and stones may break my bones, but names will never hurt me."

The title of Scott Weckerly's essay, "Free Falling," provides a framing device that doesn't begin to resonate with meaning until the metaphor appears in the final paragraph. Weckerly dramatically reveals the fear and uncertainty he experienced the day he left home for college. The significance of this familiar event deepens as readers move closer to the emotions that Weckerly reveals, and the narrative's tension doesn't yield until the final paragraph of the essay, where readers join the figurative "skydiver," take a deep breath, and jump.

Curtis Dean Adams, in "The Relationship," displays a confident storytelling voice that subtly shifts its tone from wry humor to horror as events unfold. In recounting the devastating effects of his father's murder, Adams articulates his pain yet remains in full control of his material. Rather than tagging on a conclusion that resolves the essay by summarizing its significance or moral, Adams skillfully maintains a narrative presence, enabling readers to discover and experience his meaning for themselves.

In "An Escape Journey," Abida Wali writes about her family's dramatic escape from their Soviet-occupied homeland of Afghanistan. Like Adams, she rivets readers with a close-up focus on unfolding events, compelling her audience to keep reading to find out what happens. Also like Adams, she doesn't interpret the significance of what she's experienced but instead artfully renders it within the moment—in this case, when she arrives, crying, in Pakistan, "walking backward to get one last glimpse of [her] beloved country."

Amber Sky Emanuel's "Limitless Hope" recounts her visit to Dachau, once a Nazi concentration camp, as a high school senior on a class trip to Europe. Her descriptions of the camp and its crematorium, an encounter with a middle-aged man kneeling in prayer, and a haunting photo of an emaciated prisoner enable the reader to see clearly what Emanuel saw. The subtle comparison between Emanuel's life and that of the Dachau prisoners' lives strengthens the realization that she reaches in the closing paragraphs. Ultimately, Emanuel's narrative compels its readers to remember a moment in time that should never be forgotten or ignored.

# *Sticks and Stones*

**Nicole Ball**

*Niagara University*
*Niagara University, New York*

James Nichols was short and scrawny, the smallest kid in the entire eighth grade class. But he had a foul mouth and a belligerent attitude to make up for it. And he was a bully. 1

James sat in the front seat of the school bus, relegated there by the bus driver after some infraction or other. The driver, a balding, heavy-set man who paid little or no attention to the charges he shuttled back and forth, rarely spoke and, except for that act of discipline, seemed disinclined to do anything else. The punishment, however, didn't seem to faze James; in fact, he reveled in it. Sitting in the front put him at the head of all the action and surrounded him with easy victims: those too timid or meek to trespass into the "tough" zone at the back of the bus. 2

I was a year older than James and, though not very tall myself, was at least a foot taller than he was. But by my last year in junior high school, I had a terrible complexion, a mouthful of braces, and a crippling shyness. I sat in the second seat on the school bus, only because I couldn't get any closer to the front. 3

My brother, Greg, who was a year younger, generally sat with me because while he was a bit shorter, and much more confident, he had no more desire to mix with the cigarette-toting crowd in the back of the bus than I did. And although we didn't always get along well at home, we both felt that it was nice to have someone to sit with on the bus, even if we didn't talk much. 4

In our junior high, as in all junior highs, skill at socializing out-ranked skill in classes. And since Greg and I were both social outcasts, we endured our share of teasing and taunts. But James Nichols set out to top them all. 5

At first, of course, his words were easy to ignore, mostly because they were nothing new. But as his taunts grew louder and nastier, he 6 developed the habit of kneeling on his seat and leaning over the back to shout his unrelenting epithets down upon us. The kids in the back of the bus relished every moment of our humiliation, often cheering him on. James puffed up with pride over his cruelty. The bus driver never said a word, though he could not have helped but hear the barrage of insults. Inside, I seethed.

"Ignore him," my parents insisted. "He'll eventually stop when he realizes that you're not going to react." Their words were well meant, but didn't help. The taunts continued and even intensified when we got to school. Upon arrival, the buses lined up in front of the school building, waiting until exactly 8:10 to release their passengers. Those long moments sitting in the parking lot, staring at the red plastic seat in front of me, praying for the bell to ring so I could escape James, were pure torture. 7

Each morning, Greg and I would flee from the bus. "I can't take this much more," I would rage under my breath. Oh how I longed to tear James to pieces. And although I knew I would never physically attack James, I felt better imagining myself doing so. Greg, though, would never respond to my frustrated exclamations, which only added to my wrath. After all, didn't he hate James too? But more often than not, I was just too furious to care what Greg might have been thinking. 8

The showdown, I suppose, was inevitable. 9

One morning as we sat in the school parking lot, James took his taunting too far. I don't remember what he said, but I remember what he did. He pulled a long, slender wooden drumstick from his pocket. He started to tap Greg on the top of the head, each hit emphasizing every syllable of his hateful words. My brother stared straight ahead. James laughed. The kids in the back of the bus laughed. The bus driver ignored everything. 10

My anger boiled over. "Don't you touch him!" I shrieked, striking out and knocking the drumstick from James's hand. At that moment, I didn't care that my parents had advised us to ignore James. I didn't care that everyone turned to gape at me. I didn't care that even the bus driver glanced up from his stony reverie. I only wanted James to leave my brother alone. As the stick clattered to the floor, audible in the sudden silence, I bit my lip, uncertain of what I had done and afraid of what might result. 11

My mistake, of course, was thinking my screams would end the taunts. The crowd at the back of the bus waited to see James's reaction. With his authority threatened, James turned on me like a viper. 12

"Shut up, bitch!" he hissed. Coming from a home where "shut up" was considered strong language, James's swear word seemed the worst of all evils.

My eyes wide, I shuddered but didn't respond. Words were words, and if I had done nothing else, at least I had caused the bully to revert to words instead of actions. I turned my face to the window, determined to ignore his insults for the few remaining minutes before school. But a movement from Greg caught my eye, and I looked back. 13

In one swift movement, Greg reached into the front seat, grabbed James by the coat, yanked him out into the aisle, pulled him down, and delivered two quick, fierce jabs to James's face. Then he released him without a word and settled back into his seat. James, for once in his life, was speechless. His cheek flaming red from where the blows had struck, he stared at my brother without moving until the bus driver clicked open the doors a moment later, indicating we could go into school. 14

My parents heard about the incident, of course, and called the assistant principal about the entire matter. When the vice principal questioned my brother, Greg's explanation was simple: "He called Nicole a swear word, and no one calls my sister that." Greg had never said anything more touching. 15

I have heard it said that violence never solves anything, and it didn't. The bus driver was advised to keep an eye on James, but no admonition would have spurred the driver to interfere in anything. The teasing went on, cruel as ever, until James threatened to slit our throats with a knife he swore he had hidden in his locker at school. After that, even though a locker search turned up nothing, my parents drove us to school every morning, and my mother talked to us about what to do if James ever pulled a knife on us at school. 16

But for me an imagined weapon paled when compared with the vivid memory of the complete silence on the bus, the blazing red mark on James's face, the calm little smile that tugged at the edges of my brother's mouth, and the click of the bus doors as they opened to free us. 17

# *Free Falling*

**Scott Weckerly**

*Southern Illinois University, Carbondale*
*Carbondale, Illinois*

The impact of saying good-bye and actually leaving did not hit me until the day of my departure. Its strength woke me an hour before my alarm clock would, as for the last time Missy, my golden retriever, greeted me with a big, sloppy lick. I hated it when she did that, but that day I welcomed her with open arms. I petted her with long, slow strokes, and her sad eyes gazed into mine. Her coat felt more silky than usual. Of course, I did not notice any of these qualities until that day, which made me all the more sad about leaving her. 1

The entire day was like that: a powerful awakening of whom and what I would truly miss. I became sentimental about saying good-bye to many people I had taken for granted—the regulars who came into the restaurant where I worked, the ones I never seemed to find time to speak with. I had to leave all of my friends and also the classmates I had always intended to "get to know someday." Most important, I would be forced to say farewell to the ones who raised me. 2

All at once, the glorious hype about becoming independent and free became my sole, frightening reality. I began to feel the pressure of all my big talk about being a big shot going to a big-time school. Big deal. I had waited so impatiently for the day to arrive, and now that it finally had, I felt as if I did not want to go. I suppose that goes with the territory of enrolling in a university six hours from home. 3

Upon my decision to do so, in fact, all of my personal problems had seemed to fade. I didn't care; I was leaving. I wanted to make it clear to everyone that I *wanted* to go—and by God, I was ready. Then the day came, and I wondered if I was honestly ready to go. 4

My dad and stepmom were taking me to school, but first I had to say good-bye to my mom. No one ever said divorce was easy. I met Mom for brunch that morning, and she immediately began talking of my future experiences. More so, she talked a little of her 5 first year away from home—cluttered dorm, shy roommate, some art history classes—and she spoke with such detail and enthusiasm that I clearly saw what a lasting impression college makes. We talked then of my expectations—what the guys on my floor would be like, how I hoped my classes would not be on opposite sides of campus, whether I'd gain weight on cafeteria food.

She paused for a second, and then quipped, "The food won't make you gain weight; the beer will." 6

I smiled. I felt relieved that Mom was in a cheerful mood. Ironically, the sky was filled with sunshine and bright, silky clouds. Somehow, I'd expected it to be gray and overcast. As we talked, I realized I would soon begin the long, complicated road to independence. The security I had selfishly taken for granted at home would eventually diminish into memory. Home would no longer be home; it would be Carbondale, Illinois. 7

When the waitress brought our bill, Mom's mood shifted noticeably. She became quiet, even somber. I suppose for her that somehow signaled the conclusion of our last meal together, at least the last one for quite some time. She looked down at the table pensively. Looking back now, I can see the significance that day probably had for my mother. As a parent, she must have been anticipating that day ever since the day I was born, and it surely challenged her emotionally. 8

She walked me to my car, and I could feel my sadness in the pit of my stomach. The summer breeze dried my eyes, and I blinked profusely to moisten them. 9

"Well, I guess I have to go," I mumbled, looking into the distance. I could not believe I did not have the courage to say that directly into her eyes. 10

"I know," she replied with a faint smile and then quipped, "It's not too late to change your mind." She was joking, but there seemed to be some seriousness in her voice. Her smile quickly faded when I said I couldn't. 11

"I'm going to miss you," she added. 12

"You make it sound as if you're never going to see me again." 13

"You could call . . . collect, of course." 14

I laughed. The implication that all the money I would spend from then on would be my own was scary, yet funny as well. 15

"Don't worry about me too much, Mom." 16

"I'll miss you." She drew me close and gave me a hug, and I assured her I'd be back sooner than she'd realize. She then told me that she loved me. 17

"I . . . love you, too." The difficulty of saying those words overwhelmed me. I had always seen myself as someone with solid, untouchable emotions. At that moment, though, I was in a fragile, quivering state; and I could not believe I had conjured such a false image of myself. 18

We drew apart, and I slowly climbed into my gray Maxima. Mom did not cry, but who knows what happened when I turned the corner. I don't think I want to know. 19

At that time, I felt like a rookie sky diver preparing for his first plunge. The cabin door opens to reveal the extreme distance of his fall, which leads to either sheer excitement or eventual death. The naïveté that sheltered his fear disappears at the sudden reality of the moment. By then, of course, it is much too late to turn back. The very thought that this was *his* idea seems absurd to him, and he feels like the only person on the face of the planet. And so he closes his eyes, takes a deep breath, and jumps. 20

# *The Relationship*

**Curtis Dean Adams**

*Augusta State University*
*Augusta, Georgia*

*Revenge his foul and most unnatural murder.*
— William Shakespeare, *Hamlet*

As the new year of 1973 approached, I was a thirteen-year-old boy living in an ugly brown-and-white aluminum mobile home attached to a huge, highway-safety–yellow fireworks store. It was surrounded by twelve miles of stinking swamps and saltwater marshes; these were infested with mosquitoes, wild boars, and alligators. Man, I was happy. I had my dog, my books, a semiautomatic .22 rifle with a telescopic sight, and access to enough explosives to blow up a small country. To most other boys my age, mine was an enviable position. As eldest child, and only boy, I also enjoyed the privilege and solace of wandering through the swamps whenever the spirit moved me. 1

We had been living in the swamps for a year and a half. From the suburbs of Augusta, my father relocated us to this smelly, low-country wasteland (whose major crops were methane and poisonous snakes). The reason for the move was financial. We would be fleecing Yankees on their yearly migrations to and from Florida. This, it turned out, was easily accomplished by selling them an endless variety of tacky items: fireworks, pecan rolls, sexist beach towels, life-size rubber snakes, tapestries of dogs playing poker, and velvet paintings of either Elvis or Jesus (I'm not sure who was more popular). 2

Our store was named Crazy Cecil's, although my father's name was not Cecil, and he wasn't crazy. It was huge, brightly lit, and packed to overflowing with worthless items. Like flies drawn to garbage, people stopped at our store and couldn't seem to help themselves. We raked in so much of their money that we soon opened two more stores on the same deserted stretch of Highway 17. 3

But our prosperity and our troubles were soon received in equal measure. Evidently, because our stores were the biggest and the tackiest, we were running our local competition out of business. And, understandably, our local competitors were not enthusiastic about the trend continuing. I discovered this when, in late November, I woke to the sounds of cussing and falling boxes. I ran through the dark trailer and into the store as my father finished extinguishing a burning stack of boxes filled with moccasins. 4

"What happened?" 5

"Somebody threw a bomb through the window." 6

"Why?" 7

"To blow us up, damn it; now go see to your mother." 8

I stared in amazement. 9

"Move, boy!" my father shouted. 10

I moved, since I knew it wasn't smart to make my father repeat a command. I found my mother, face in hands, in their bedroom. 11

"Why would someone want to kill us?" I asked. 12

"Honey," she said softly, "we're making lots of money here. Before we came here other people were making that money." 13

"Like the Tylers," I said matter-of-factly. 14

The Tylers, none of whom I had met, were a family who owned a much smaller store a few miles up the highway. Having built newer stores on either side of them, we were slowly squeezing the life out of the Tylers' business. 15

Slow on the uptake, I would never be a detective. "You mean the Tylers did this?" 16

"Yes, I'm sure they must have," Mom said. She was looking at me with a calm, sad pity in her eyes that I didn't understand. 17

I was mad and ready to fight. "Why did they do it?" 18

"Honey, I'm sure the Tylers would like us to leave, so they could make the money they were making before we came." 19

"Well, that's too bad," I said. 20

"Yes," she said, "and I'm certain your hardheaded father feels the same way." 21

The funny thing is, it took the police six hours to show up that night. I sensed that something wasn't right. 22

The next day, my father told me that we had been quite lucky. The "bomb," a Molotov cocktail, was a bottle of gasoline with a gas-soaked rag tied around the neck for a fuse. As the bottle came through the window, the lighted rag caught on the glass and slipped 23 off the bottle. "Had it not," my father informed me, "son, we wouldn't be having this little talk."

While my father seemed worried by this turn of events, I was not. I had faith in my father's ability to handle any situation. 24

An imposing figure, my father stood well over six feet. His jet black hair and red beard, though neatly trimmed, gave him the look of a pirate. His green eyes burned with the fire of a man who had sold his soul and wanted to get his money's worth before the bill came due. Large-boned and muscular, he was built like a linebacker, yet he moved with the smoothness of the high school basketball player he had been at one time. He was big, good-looking, and as slick as boiled okra, and he knew it. 25

My father had also been in the army for a brief time and served as a sergeant in an armored unit. Like the biggest dog on the street, Curtis Senior loved a face-off. In 1972, the phrase "I'm sorry, but you can't smoke here" was virtually unknown. Now and then, when my father would spot some large, mean-looking man smoking in the store, he would tell me, "Watch this." And, with a huge cigar clenched in his teeth, my father would slowly stride over to the man in question and say, "You can't smoke in here." 26

The man in question would look at him incredulously and say, "You're smokin'," at which point I could smell testosterone from fifty feet away. 27

"My store," Dad would say. 28

Then they would glare at each other for a few timeless seconds, and my father would smile his slow smile as the man of the day, sometimes cussing, sometimes not, would finally put his cigarette out on the floor. For my father, the youngest of six boys from a dirt-poor Kentucky family, that sort of head-butting was what he thought of as a good time. 29

Then, on New Year's Eve, 1972, my father faced off with someone who wasn't as inclined to back down. 30

On that New Year's Eve, I was outside among the large, yellow billboards and flashing lights on the road, playing with an assortment of loose fireworks. It was cool that night but not brisk. The swamps were dormant, and the stench of a paper mill hung in the air. 31

SWISSTH . . . CRACK! SWISSTH . . . CRACK! Bottle rockets flew into the air. Depending on the accuracy of the fuse, I was able to come within a few feet of cars traveling the highway a hundred yards away, although I had stopped targeting cars a few months before when one of my targets turned out to be a state patrol cruiser. 32

SWISSTH . . . CRACK! 33

A couple of weeks before that New Year's, as we hurried to open our third store, Looney Luke's, a second firebombing occurred. But because the new store hadn't been stocked yet, and because my father possessed the foresight to use a double-wide fireproof mobile home as a building, the fire caused little damage. We simply repainted, stocked the shelves, and were ready for the New Year's rush. "That'll show those stupid sandlappers," my father had said, pleased with the lack of damage. 34

SWISSTH . . . CRACK! 35

SWISSTH . . . CRACK! I looked at my watch—two hours till the new year. My father was at the other store, and I wondered what was going on there—seven miles down the road. I thought about the bomb threat we had received that very evening. 36

SWISSTH . . . CRACK! 37

"Dean! Dean!" My mother called to me from the store, her voice thin, cracked, urgent. I ran into my nightmare. 38

Inside the trailer, I found my younger sisters, Robin and Ginger, ages eight and seven, wailing uncontrollably as my mother fumbled with their clothing. Toni, age ten, was already dressed. She stood blank-faced as if someone had stolen her brain. My mother's face quivered, as if it were ready to explode into a million pieces. 39

"The hospital called. Your father's been shot," she said, her voice skirting the edge of hysteria. She might as well have slapped me full force across the face. 40

"Is he all right?" I asked, barely managing to pull the question from my mouth. 41

"They won't say over the phone. They want us to come down." 42

That was when someone stole my brain. 43

My mother loaded us into the station wagon and drove her cargo of quiet, stunned children south, down Highway 17 toward Savannah. 44

We arrived at the hospital emergency entrance. Dazed, I floated in with the rest of the family. As we entered the hospital, one nurse took our mother from us as another sat us down. We were quiet, still in shock. Two or ten minutes later, I can't remember, a nurse led us down a sterile tunnel to a large, empty, dimly lit, gray-tiled room. There stood our mother and two nurses. One of the nurses had her eyes fixed on mine. I could tell she was about to speak. 45

"Your father is dead," she said. 46

My mouth opened, and I took in every ounce of air in that room with a sound no child should be able to make; the nurse opened her 47 arms, and I fell in. With the exhalation of my breath, my soul became a river of sound and tears. That nurse wrapped her arms around me with the strength of steel straps on a powder keg.

I must have cried myself out, for after that night, I didn't shed 48
another tear for two days, until, at the surreal, open-casket wake, I thought I saw my father breathe and had to be taken, screaming, from the room.

When we got home from the hospital, a flock of detectives were 49
waiting for us. They explained that my father had been killed by a bullet from a high-powered rifle while he and his partner were standing in the parking lot of the newest store. The assassins had been parked across the highway in a black Cadillac, and they were gone before my dad's partner could figure out how to switch the rifle he was carrying off the safety position. The detectives said it had been a professional job.

A black Cadillac? 50

Hired assassins? 51

Had we been propelled into the television world? 52

The detectives wanted us to pack quickly so that they could 53
move us to a motel where they felt we would be safer.

"I need a gun," I said, starting for my father's pistols. 54

"No," said my mother in a quiet but firm voice. 55

"Yes," I said, matching her tone. And I meant it. 56

"Son," someone said, "there's no need for that. If these people 57
want you dead, you're dead."

Very comforting words. 58

We left Savannah the next day in a chartered plane bound for 59
Kentucky.

At Slate Hill Baptist Church, we buried my father's body on a 60
high hill overlooking the now snow-covered, rolling pastures of the southeastern Kentucky landscape. It seemed the perfect place to be buried. London, Kentucky, the hometown of my father, mother, and me. Those hills had some inexplicable hold on my soul, maybe because "our people" had lived there since the country's first push westward.

The weather was ideal that day: cold, overcast, with large 61
snowflakes falling slowly to the ground. As I followed too closely behind the dark suits carrying my father's casket to the grave, I felt my mother's hand on my shoulder pulling me back to her. I recalled that while she was in college, her father had been murdered in a chance encounter with an escaped convict. She knew the drill.

That day I had thought my relationship with my father was over. I was a presumptuous thirteen-year-old. 62

A few days after the funeral, I remembered sitting under a pecan tree at school, six months before his murder, as a friend told me about his own father's death in a motorcycle accident and how the event had ripped his life apart. I had thought about my relationship with my father, and on that day, I had determined that if my father died, it wouldn't be a big deal. Wrong again. 63

My father's murder stole my sanity as well as the sanity of my entire family. Our house became a zoo without a keeper. Our mother opened a restaurant and had to work countless hours every week, leaving her four children ample time at home to scream and fight in our wild frustration. Toni locked herself in her bedroom for a period of five years and was rarely seen leaving it except to attend her Evangelic Baptist Church. I wanted to be more help to my family, but I was too angry, too bitter, and too wild—an animal trapped and gnawing off my own leg to get free from the trap. I couldn't stop feeling my father's eyes upon me. I begged my mother to send me to a military academy for eighth grade; my soul screamed for order. But I was able to find no escape in a uniform; my storm was internal, and I couldn't run away from myself or my father. 64

His ghost haunted me in various ways for years: nightmares, fear that kept me sleeping with a gun under my pillow, disapproval I perceived in the eyes of adult men. I would dream of his return, his walking through the door, saying, "Why haven't you avenged my murder?" It was in the houses of my fellow teenage friends that I was most uncomfortable; I saw my father's disapproval in their fathers' eyes. 65

In my senior year of high school, the theater found me, and there I found some diversion from my inner turmoil. Around three o'clock in the morning, in an empty theater, while working on a lighting design, I had just related something about my father's nasty temper when my friend Gershon, looking down at me from a twenty-five-foot ladder, said, "You didn't like your father very much, did you?" At that moment, Gershon fired a diamond bullet and placed it squarely between my eyes. I had not liked my father when I was thirteen, but, I had thought, what boy does? His murder had relieved the tension of misunderstanding between us. I had been glad he was gone all those years, allowing me to become (however screwed-up) who I was. This hidden guilt had been my chain. 66

And that marked the beginning of the healing. It was ten years after his murder that Gershon's truth began to scrape the scales from 67 my eyes. Many difficult years and conflicting emotions lay ahead. Now, more than twenty years after his death, wondering what form our relationship would have taken were he still alive, I look in the morning mirror and give a wry smile as I notice the blue eyes my mother gave me slowly turning into the green of my father's.

Standing in the wings during a recent production of *Hamlet*, 68
I shuddered hearing Hamlet tell his father's ghost what I would tell mine: "Rest, rest, perturbed spirit!"

# *An Escape Journey*

**Abida Wali**

*University of California, San Diego*
*La Jolla, California*

1 It was 11:30 p.m. in Kabul. We were all waiting for my uncle to return from a meeting with his collaborators. Every night before the curfew, they distributed *Shabnameh* (*The Night Letter*), a pamphlet mimeographed or copied by hand and secretly left in public places. Many people had been arrested, tortured, imprisoned, and killed for the possession or distribution of antiregime *Night Letters.* Usually, my uncle got home by ten, but now the clock was about to strike twelve midnight. What could have happened? Had he been arrested? If he didn't get home before the midnight curfew went into effect, he could be shot.

2 Suddenly, a pounding at the door broke the silence. My heart beat faster and faster as I rushed to the door. Who could it be? Could it be my uncle—or soldiers coming to arrest my dad after they arrested my uncle?

3 "Who is it?" I asked.

4 "Open the door," a voice I didn't recognize replied from the other side of the door.

5 "Open the door," the voice repeated.

6 As I turned the knob, the person pushed the door open, throwing me back against the wall. My uncle rushed into the living room. I slammed the door and ran after him. Trembling and gasping, he looked toward my dad and said, "Abdulla and Ahmed have been arrested . . . they could have given my name under torture . . . I'm next."

7 "We have to leave immediately," my dad replied.

8 I helped my mom pack canned foods, clothing, and the first-aid kit. We were told to take only the things that we would need for our journey, but Mom slipped the family photo album between the clothes. After a frantic hour of rushing from room to room, gathering our supplies in bundles, we had to wait until the curfew was lifted

at dawn. At the crack of dawn, we abandoned the house forever, setting out on an uncertain journey. As Mom shut the front door, she looked for the last time at her great-grandmother's teapot.

We took a bus from Kabul to Nangarhar. Along the road to 9
Nangarhar were two or three checkpoints where soldiers would search the bus for arms and illegal documents. At the first checkpoint, a soldier got on the bus. From the hammer and sickle on his cap, I knew he was a Soviet. He wore a big army coat and held a rifle, an AK-47 Kalashnikov, to his chest. His boots shook and rattled the windows and the metal floor of the bus. Suddenly, he stopped, pointed his gun at a man, and signaled him to get off the bus. The man ignored him. The soldier stepped forward and tried to pull him out of the seat, but the man clung to the seat and wouldn't let go. My heart was racing. Drops of sweat were forming on my forehead. Finally, the man let go and was escorted by two other soldiers to a jeep parked beside the bus. The pounding of the boots against the bus floor started again, and this time, the soldier stopped at my dad and me.

"Where are you going?" he asked. 10

"To my uncle's funeral in Nangarhar," Dad answered. 11

"Your ID?" 12

Dad gave him his ID. The soldier opened it to see the picture. 13
I felt a drop of sweat drop from my forehead. Finally, the soldier handed back the ID. He looked around the bus once more and gave the driver permission to pass.

We made the rest of the journey in fear of getting blown up by 14
antipersonnel mines. I saw six passenger buses that had been destroyed by mines on the road to Nangarhar. Finally, after eight hours of traveling, which should have been four, we reached Nangarhar.

From the bus station we took a taxi to a friend's house and 15
waited there two days for someone to smuggle us across the border. After two days, my dad's friend introduced us to the Smuggler. His six-foot height, bushy beard, upturned moustache, and dark eyebrows made him look dreadful. He wore baggy trousers and heavy red-leather slippers with upturned toes, and he had a carbine slung over his back. He was a Pathan. The Pathans, an Afghan ethnic group, are warriors who obey neither God nor man. Their law is the law of the rifle and the knife. He told us that he could take only three or four people at a time. My parents decided that I should go with my aunt and uncle.

We had to dress like the Pathan peasants who lived near the bor- 16
der so that our western clothes did not advertise the fact that we

were from the capital and trying to escape. My uncle dressed like the Smuggler. My aunt and I were given very heavy dresses with colorful patterns, sequins, and dangling jewelry. In addition, outside the city, the women were obliged to wear a Chaderi, a veil through which we could see but not be seen. It comes in three colors: yellowish brown, gray, and blue. Ours were yellowish brown.

We left the house at dawn and walked a mile or two to reach the main road. While walking, the Chaderi twisted and clung to my legs. As I looked down to unwrap it, I stumbled over a rock and fell to the ground, injuring my right knee slightly. It burned, but I managed to catch up with my aunt and uncle and acted like nothing had happened. After a short time, a lorry arrived for us, and we spent the next few hours with sheep and goats, covering our faces with a piece of cloth to keep the smell and the dust out. 17

The sound of a helicopter approaching got our attention. It was an MI-24, a kind of armored helicopter that the Soviets used to bombard villages, agricultural fields, and mosques. We feared that this time we might be its target, but fortunately it passed us. After a few minutes, we came upon a village. From a small opening in the side of the lorry, I witnessed the aftermath of a bombardment. The air attack had reduced the village to rubble, and those who survived it were running around shouting and screaming. An agricultural field outside the village was burned to ashes, and a pall of smoke and dust drifted over the valley. The images of those people and their ruined village haunted us the rest of our journey. 18

After a few hours, the lorry stopped, and the driver opened the gate and called, "Last stop." Holding the Chaderi, I jumped to the ground. The desert was covered with the tracks of horses, donkeys, camels, and people. There were many groups of people traveling in caravans: young orphaned boys; a lonely man with a sad expression on his face, all of his possessions packed on top of a camel; and numerous donkeys carrying women while their husbands walked alongside. We were all on our way to Pakistan. 19

As we waited for our donkeys, my uncle whispered to me, "The Smuggler is a government agent, a Militia." My heart skipped a beat. I knew exactly what that meant—he would turn us in. The government recruits tribesmen like the Smuggler for undercover assignments. The Smuggler was talking with some other people, looking at us as he spoke. When he started to walk toward us, I thought my life was over. I wanted to scream and run. He stopped and signaled my uncle to come. As they walked toward a mud hut in the distance, my 20 whole life flashed in front of my eyes. I saw my school, my parents, my execution.

"Did they take him for interrogation?" I asked myself. I could see the hut, and I wondered what was going on inside. When my uncle came out the door, I ran to him. He had been bargaining for the price of the mules. We rented four mules and set out with the caravan. 21

Riding that mule was an experience that I will never forget. It was hard to stay balanced with the heavy dress and the veil, especially once we began to climb a mountain. The trail was just wide enough for the mule to put down his hooves. As we turned and twisted along the mountainside, I wondered whether I should close my eyes, to try to shut out the danger, or keep them open, to be prepared when we fell down the side of the mountain. But the mule was surefooted, and I didn't fall. I learned that if I could relax, I would not fall off. 22

The hot summer sun was right above our heads, and my mouth was completely dry. We could see a village at the bottom of the mountain—four hours away, according to the Smuggler. After a few minutes, however, we got to a small lake. The water was yellow and covered with algae, but the Smuggler drank it and then brought me a cupful. As I looked into the cup, I was reminded of the solution that we prepared in biology class in order to grow bacteria. This lake was the main source of water for the village. God knows what microorganisms were swimming in it. 23

"I wouldn't drink it if I were you," my aunt said. 24

But I closed my eyes and drank the whole cup at once. I would worry about the consequences later. 25

We reached the village just before sunset. After eating dinner and resting for several hours, we started to travel again. The night journey was magnificent. The sky was clear, the moon was full, and millions of stars seemed to be winking at the night travelers. We could hear the bells of another caravan coming from the opposite direction, getting louder and louder as it got close. The ding-a-ling of that caravan added a rhythm to the lonely desert. 26

Now we were in the territory of the Freedom Fighters. We knew if they recognized the Smuggler, they would execute all of us as communist spies. The Freedom Fighters and the Militia are enemies, and the Freedom Fighters did not trust anyone who was traveling with an agent. 27

At dawn we reached a small teahouse. It consisted of a large, bare room with a dirt floor partially covered by canvas mats. A few 28 small windows, with plastic in place of glass, let in a bit of light. A smoky wood fire in a tin stove served for heating and boiling water for tea. The owner brought us tea and bread, a soothing sight for restless travelers.

We walked on, and soon a signpost got my attention. As I got 29
closer, I was able to read the words: Welcome to Pakistan.

I started to cry, walking backward to get one last glimpse of my 30
beloved country.

# *Limitless Hope*

**Amber Sky Emanuel**

*Elizabethtown College*
*Elizabethtown, Pennsylvania*

The day began as had the previous three: a loud, rapid banging followed by, "Girls! Time to get up!" Since I had the longest and thickest hair and showering took me a few more minutes, I had been elected by my roommates, Jessie and Laura, to go first, so I rolled out of bed and answered with a weak, "Yeah, yeah, we're up." The two other girls were able to sleep peacefully for a few more minutes, while I hurriedly tried to bathe in a foreign shower, which consisted of a nozzle on the end of a wiggly rope that did not offer much in the way of water control. After three days of struggling, however, I had successfully gotten my shower time down to ten minutes. 1

It was Sunday, March 25, 2001, and I and about one hundred other students and parents were on the fourth day of our high school European tour. On our first day in Germany, we visited Rothenberg on der Tauber, a small, fortified town that had changed little since medieval times. For the next two days, we toured Munich, visiting its museums, churches, castles, and gardens. Today we would be driving to Dachau, the first organized concentration camp in Nazi Germany. Our tour guide for the trip was Adrian, a short Englishman, and he had already informed us that the bus ride to Dachau would be a long one. My friends and I had come to realize that being on the bus was not fun, that there was only one way to enjoy a bus ride: asleep. We got as comfortable as we could. 2

About two hours later, Adrian gently awakened us, saying he was about to start talking about Dachau. I roused my seatmate, Jason, and we began to listen groggily as Adrian spoke, "I want to give you some background information about Dachau so that your experience at the concentration camp will be more memorable." As he began his lecture, we wanted to go back to sleep. 3

Adrian began by telling us that after World War I Germany was 4
left poverty stricken; people's money was worthless. People needed suitcases full of cash just to buy a loaf of bread, and the entire country was beginning to lose hope. Suddenly, a man appeared on the political scene and told people to have hope, promising the German people that the economy, under his supervision, would flourish again. This man was Adolf Hitler. When we hear the name today, we do not associate it with hope or promise, but at that time, the German people did. He was telling people what they wanted to hear, promising them what they wanted, and because of the hope Hitler offered, they followed him.

The Germans also listened when Hitler spoke about having a 5
pure country, one populated with only those of the Aryan race, and how eliminating those who were not Aryan was necessary. Simultaneously, mass-produced propaganda was distributed explaining how Jewish people were supposedly evil. Soon, those people who spoke against Hitler's ideas were taken to Dachau. Eventually Jews, homosexuals, and other "undesirable" people were all forced into this camp together.

Few people had the courage to speak out against the atrocities 6
that were taking place. White Rose, a small college student organization, secretly spread pamphlets trying to convince others that what was happening was wrong. These students were eventually caught, tried in court, and killed. Adrian concluded his speech by asking the question, "Would you have been brave enough?" He also reminded us, "There is always hope." For the final ten minutes of the bus ride we sat in silence, digesting what we had just been told and contemplating Adrian's question.

The bus rolled down the road and into the gravel parking lot. 7
Jessie, Laura, and I grabbed our coats and walked out of the bus. It was misting, but we had become used to touring places in the dampness. We picked up a small map and entered Dachau.

A tall metal fence surrounded the camp. Once we passed 8
through the fence, directly to our left was the museum, which had once housed the kitchen, the laundry, storage facilities, and shower rooms. To the right were the barracks. Only two remained, replicas of the original thirty-four that had housed the camp's prisoners.

There were seventeen barracks on either side of the camp, each 9
separated from the other by a row of trees that the prisoners had planted. We walked single file down a path, gravel crunching beneath our feet, past where the barracks, each marked by a wooden plank

outline, had once stood. Every day, prisoners had walked this same path. We walked past the memorial barracks in silence. As we moved down the path, I carefully sidestepped the puddles that had been created from the recent rain, trying to keep my jeans from soaking up the water. I thought about the prisoners who would have had to make this walk in the cold and damp in light clothing and badly torn shoes, not allowed to sidestep the puddles.

We were now at the end of the camp. There was a break in the 10
tall wire fencing, through which we walked. The trees outside were
large and in bloom, and a small wooden bridge helped us cross a
babbling brook; the scene was pretty. When I learned that the crema-
toriums were beyond the bridge, the beauty of this country scene
seemed overwhelmingly ironic. I wondered if the prisoners were
aware that when they heard this babbling brook, saw these beautiful
trees, and crossed this pretty bridge, they would not be returning.

The first building we entered had four rooms. The last room had 11
old wooden floorboards and falling white plaster. There was only one
other person in it when we entered. He was a middle-aged man with
a single rose. We had seen these red roses, in the three previous
rooms, but flowers were spread all over the camp as makeshift
memorials. This man went down on his knees and carefully placed
the rose against the wall. He began to pray in an unfamiliar language
but soon had to stop because he was weeping.

The three of us quickly exited, leaving the man in peace, and 12
walked to the next building. The doors at the front of this building
were open, and when we stepped beneath the roof, we found our-
selves facing the ovens. There were two ovens. Their doors were
open, as if only time had stopped their "work." Even though I tried
hard not to, I could imagine prisoners being pushed into the flames.
The incomprehensible fear of being burned alive overwhelmed me.
I stared at the open ovens—mouths of death—thinking about all
the innocent people who had been murdered. Emotions flashed
through me: anger, guilt, sympathy, fear, and helplessness.

We each left the crematorium with tears freely flowing down our 13
faces. We walked across the bridge again in silence. This time I no-
ticed a barricade of barbed wire a couple feet down the stream. The
stream did not have the same appeal as when I had first crossed it.

We walked down the path again. So many thoughts were 14
swirling around in my head, but I realized I needed time to think
about what I was seeing before I was ready to discuss it with my
friends. I think the others felt the same. We walked quietly into one

of the barracks. Inside were the crudely made bunk beds. There was no doubt that sleeping conditions were deplorable, especially considering each barracks contained as many as 1,600 prisoners—a thousand more than the buildings were originally designed to hold. I found that imagining hundreds of men living together in these cramped quarters was difficult; I felt guilty about complaining about the shower in my hotel room.

The museum, the last building we entered, contained large pic- 15
tures of prisoners. Captions were written entirely in German, but captions were not needed to understand these pictures. Prisoners were so malnourished that their bones were visible. One picture was of an elderly man; his clothes hung, as if they were several sizes too large, from his emaciated body. His head was shaved like all prisoners' and he was seated at a table doing some menial labor. He looked directly at the camera when the picture was taken. His eyes were filled with despair and pleading.

Twenty minutes into the return bus ride I fell asleep. The day 16
had been emotionally draining. Many unanswered questions and disturbing thoughts lingered in my head. In response to Adrian's question, I had come to the conclusion that I would have not been brave enough to do anything. I am sometimes too afraid to speak in class, afraid of giving a wrong answer. How could I have been brave enough—strong enough—to stand against many people in stating my beliefs? Besides the overwhelming feeling of sadness for what the prisoners had to endure, I also was amazed. The strength, both physical and emotional, of all of the prisoners was astonishing. While millions died during this time, others *did* survive. And they survived despite the best efforts of others to kill them. Why did so many people have to die? That is an impossible question for one to answer. For those who lived through this terrible era, maybe they survived because they had hope. Sixty years later, people still hope. Continually faced with challenges, though not as dire as those who were sent to Dachau, we all hold on to those strands of hope, and when I think of the solitary man praying, I imagine he was praying for the hope that someday people will be brave enough to step forward to stop all injustices against all human beings.

# 3 *Remembering People*

Writing about people transforms them, for when we put someone on the page the close examination that comes with writing about that person unearths surprises and reveals facets of the individual—and ourselves—that would otherwise remain hidden. Fundamental to an essay on a remembered person is a vivid portrait of the individual; through descriptions, dialogue, and anecdotes, writers make three-dimensional and lively what might otherwise be flat and stale. Yet what ultimately makes the subject of a remembered-person essay come to life is his or her importance to the writer. The four essays in this chapter, instead of settling for an easy surface description, probe, reflect, and examine the patterns that reveal the human personality and soul of their subjects—those layers of others and ourselves that rarely show up on first glance.

In "Gail," Hope Goldberg weaves memory and reflection into a pattern that illuminates the interior of her childhood dance teacher by presenting the details of her exterior—speech, appearance, manners, and actions. Goldberg subtly brings herself onto the page as well, blending Gail's life with her own in the final image of the cookie cutter, which reveals the thread of significance the writer seeks: in this image, two lives become one.

In "Only She," Erick Young uses a technique similar to Goldberg's, capturing the external details of manner and speech to present a vivid portrait of Mrs. K, also a teacher. Young, too, brings himself onto the page and portrays Mrs. K in the context of their student-teacher relationship. The rich portrait that emerges is the product of the writer's quiet and careful examination of his subject—exactly the kind of writerly move that Mrs. K, appropriately, would have expected.

In "Big Al," Therron Love remembers his uncle and mentor, Big Al, a man with a physically dominating presence whom readers are not likely to forget. Love, using vivid, clarifying details and recollections, describes the development of their relationship over nearly two decades. Although Love thinks that he is the sole beneficiary of the relationship, there comes a moment, so unexpected, when he is able to repay Big Al's kindness in full.

In "The Eyes in the Mirror," Angel Nguyen explores her guarded relationship with her grandmother. The descriptions Nguyen provides and the conversations and narrative events she recalls enable the reader to understand Nguyen's grandmother as a wellspring of Vietnamese culture and history, a connection to a world of which Nguyen is a part because of her heritage, but of which she knows little. In her final paragraph, readers—as well as the writer—discover that the relationship between Nguyen and her grandmother was not as tentative as she had once believed.

# *Gail*

**Hope Goldberg**

*University of Cincinnati*
*Cincinnati, Ohio*

She used to make toe-shoe cookies and hand them out after dance class from a tin that had been used Christmas after Christmas. Never mind that everyone else made cookies in the shapes of Christmas trees or stars. Her Christmas toe-shoe cookies had pink icing where the satin and ribbons went, and she even used little gold candy balls to decorate the tip of the slipper, the part you would stand on if your feet had been inside those cookies. The instep was shaped perfectly (as she would have shaped all our feet), probably because she made the cookie cutter herself and had free creative license with the design. "Have a cookie," she would offer, "but only one . . . you look like you've put on a couple of pounds." She would smile generously as we filed past, one by one, taking our single cookie ration. She, of course, could eat pasta, cookies, all sorts of fattening things and never gain an ounce. And she did. Constantly. 1

At fifty-plus years old, she was five foot two and weighed a mere ninety-four pounds. Her body was like a sixteen-year-old's, and were it not for her slightly wrinkled skin and graying blonde hair, she could easily have passed for a teenager. 2

Gail and her husband, Walter, lived with Gail's mother—"Mummy," she used to call her. I considered this one of her artistic affectations, like calling Walter "Darling" and the way she pursed her lips to kiss the air between one's cheek and ear when greeting a person. These seemed appropriate remnants of her glamorous performing career. Her home was filled with relics and autographed photos of famous dancers. "To Gail, with Love, George" was scrawled on a picture of Balanchine taken in the 1930s. Her life was spread out in dance symbols from one end of the house to the other. It seemed to me such a fantasy, a marvelous and unusual and exotic life. She often invited me to visit her, which always made me feel special and 3 honored. “Shhh,” she sometimes whispered as I entered. “Mummy’s sleeping. She hasn’t been feeling well lately.” I nodded my head in agreement, not daring to make a sound until we had moved silently into another room to talk. In one fluid movement, she scooped up Suki, the youngest of her beloved Siamese cats, then stroked her as long as Suki would allow. “Did I ever tell you about the time I worked with Danny Kaye at Radio City Music Hall?” she asked, her eyes focusing dreamily into the distance as she reminisced. “He was delightful to work with, a very smart and funny man. . . .” I absorbed these stories with a mixture of wonder and envy. Her life began to take on epic proportions during these sessions. She had been a dancer all her life, and to my young eyes she was everything I wanted to be. I listened and imagined myself on those stages with Balanchine, Tallchief, Fonteyn.

4 In class she was relentless. “You have to force the turnout,” she would demand. “Close the fifth. Tighter!” She had come from a generation of dancers for whom sacrifice and pain were the badges of honor, and suffering for one’s art was the ultimate reward for ambition. We accepted this, silently and courageously, as we did all her criticisms. “Anissa,” she yelled, “from the waist up you really look like a dancer. You have great feeling.” I was crushed because this meant to me that I obviously did not look like a dancer from the waist down. I wondered how I could possibly have lived this long being only half of what I so longed to be. I hated my short, heavy legs, so unlike those in the pictures of New York City Ballet dancers on the walls of Gail’s house. Those were the standards by which we were judged. I’m sure to this day that she meant to be nice, but half-good, half-murderous compliments were a regular occurrence in our classes. Thank God I wasn’t the heaviest dancer in the class and that I had some redeeming qualities in her eyes. I had feeling. I just had to pound my body into submission. And I knew I could do it.

5 When I was about thirteen and needed to dance every day to become a professional, Gail gave me a work/scholarship because my parents couldn’t afford tuition. This meant I had to help clean the studio (I had seen Gail push the big dust mop around the studio floor a million times, so I knew that part) and demonstrate for the beginning classes. She would tell me secrets about teaching: “You have to let the little ones have fun,” she confided. “You’ve got to get them hooked on ballet” (she would place the accent on the first syllable, BAL-let) “before you can make them work hard. They have to like it first. If you work them too hard, you’ll lose them.” I nodded

in agreement, realizing that I probably would have had them slaving at technique and would have surely lost all of them.

Once I asked her why she and Walter didn't have children. It seemed strange to me (having come from a family of five kids) that she should be childless. "I've never wanted any children," she replied with total candor. "I have all of you. What would I want with children of my own? Just a lot of diapers and mess. I've got so much to do; I'm much too busy." It was true. There was choreography to create, classes to prepare, music to select, costumes to design, and paperwork to complete. Gail ran a business and took care of her aging mother, emphysemic husband, and all of her students. We were her world. 6

When I was sixteen, Gail coached me for a major part in *Cinderella.* We spent hours alone in the studio, working on every detail of interpretation. "Slowly . . ." she coaxed, "gently. That's it. . . . Don't rush the music. . . . Let it lead you into the arabesque, yes, that's it. . . . Beautiful, Anissa!" I could feel her reach deep inside of me, drawing out my best performance with a sensitive combination of encouragement and criticism. Near the end of these rehearsals, Gail gave me a book on ballet terminology that she had carefully copied by hand in ink when she was very young. She had even copied the drawings of body positions and facings, how to hold one's hands, one's fingers, one's head. Every detail had been meticulously reproduced. She had kept it all her life, and now she was giving it to me. "I want you to have this," she said, pressing the book into my hands firmly, "and some day you will pass it on to one of your students, too." 7

Years later, when I started my own ballet school, I was determined to encourage my students toward a whole life. "You must go to college," I insisted. "There is a world other than dance." I gave them gifts from my heart—love, support, encouragement—but at Christmastime, without fail, my students' favorite gifts were the toe-shoe cookies with pink icing and gold candy balls I made with Gail's handmade cookie cutter. 8

# *Only She*

**Erick Young**

*University of California, San Diego*
*La Jolla, California*

1 Those eyes. Brown. No no, deep, dark brown. Hardly a wrinkle around them. Soft, smooth skin. And those eyebrows. Neither thick nor thin, just bold—two curves punctuating her facial expressions with a certain something. Surprise, amusement—up would shoot one of the brows, the right one I believe, just slightly, accompanied by a mischievous little smirk. Anger, irritation—up and inward shot both brows, tightly pressed, followed by a sharp "What d'ya want? Don't bother me!" She never really meant it, though; it was just her way of saying hello. Even though she wore glasses she could still see all, with or without them. Her deep, dark brown eyes were no ordinary eyes; no, within those deep wells rested a pair of magic orbs, two miniature crystal balls that could peer into your mind and read all your little thoughts. Some thought she had psychic powers. She knew what you were thinking, or at least she always seemed to know what I was thinking, even my most complex, inexplicable thoughts. And that was all that seemed to matter at the time. Only she, only Sonia Koujakian, Mrs. K.

2 I do not recall the first time I noticed her at school, but Mrs. K was not one to blend into a crowd. I would see her, tall and lean, wearing a skirt and a mauve-colored raincoat, holding a stuffed beige handbag in one hand, and a bright red coffeepot in the other, walking briskly across the school rotunda. She seemed so confident, always looking straight ahead as she walked about school. Perhaps it was her hair that first caught my eye. It was short, a mix of light brown and gray, combed slightly up—almost spiked. Not the typical sort of hairstyle for an English teacher at our school. It set her apart and made her look dynamic. Already I knew that she was somebody special.

3 The PSAT brought her into my life for the first time, in my sophomore year. Even though she was the senior English teacher,

she offered to coach any undaunted sophomores or juniors after school for the nefarious "SAT jr." Trying to be the savvy student, I joined a small group who gathered in her cove after school to practice vocabulary drills and sentence completions. Mrs. K would scold us on the finer points of grammar, giving us her "come on, get with the production" look as we reviewed our errors. Not the typical reaction from a teacher; she treated us like peers and would say to us whatever was on her mind without pretense, pleasantry, or euphemism. We could do the same, if we had the guts to try. Her casual disposition made me feel both relaxed and nervous; none of us knew how to act around her, whether to joke and tease her, or respect and honor her. We all agreed, however, that she was as down-to-earth as they come. Two years later, as an older and wiser senior, I would get a full dose of Mrs. K's personality.

My first day in Mrs. K's class left much to be desired. I entered 4
to find most of my classmates just laughing and joking. The first-day-of-school jitters had become passé, and the smugness that comes with seniordom dominated the room. It was a convention of Alfred E. Neumans, and the nonchalant air of "What Me Worry?" filled the classroom. Some students, however, sat very quietly. These were the wise ones; they'd heard about Mrs. K. Academic tensions hovered like the inevitable black storm cloud above Room 5C3. There was a small fear of the unknown and the unexpected nudging about in my stomach as I sat at the far end of the center table. Strange how this was the only classroom in the entire building to have six huge wooden tables instead of forty individual little desks; someone must have wanted it that way. For once I was not too anxious to sit up front. Suddenly the chattering diminished. Mrs. K was coming.

In she ambled, with her stuffed handbag and bright red cof- 5
feepot, wearing a skirt and the mauve raincoat; she was just as I had remembered. She scanned the room, and up went her right eyebrow. A most peculiar "I-know-what-you-are-up-to" smirk was our first greeting. Now I was nervous.

"All right, ladies and gentlemen, I want to see if you belong in 6
my class," she began. "Take out a pen and lots of paper." Pause. "Now don't get too worried over this, since you are all geniuses anyway. You know, if you've got it you've got it, if you don't. . . ." She shrugged. Pause. "Some of you know you don't really belong in here," she chided, pointing her finger, "and it's time you stopped getting put in Honors English just because you passed some silly little test in second grade. Well, now we're going to see what you can

do. Okay now, stop and think for a moment, and get those creative juices going. I want you to write me a paper telling me the origin of the English language. You can be as creative as you want. Make up something if you have to—two cavemen grunting at each other, I don't care. You have until the end of the period. Go."

It was not the most encouraging welcome. For a moment the whole class just sort of slumped in their seats, drained suddenly of all vitality and hopes of a relaxed senior year. Blank faces abounded, mine included. I had no idea what to write. The origin of the English language? Being "creative" seemed too risky. What ever happened to the good ol' five-paragraph essay with specific examples? Well, I didn't have any specific examples anyway. I remember staring at a sheet of white paper, then scrawling down some incoherent mumbo-jumbo. I wanted to impress her, too much. "It was nice knowing you," I sighed as I handed in my paper. What a first day. 7

Fortunately, that first day with Mrs. K would not be my last. Although the class size shrunk over the following days, as some students ran for their academic lives, I was not prepared to leave. I knew Mrs. K's class would be an arduous English journey that I could not miss; it would be a journey well worth taking. 8

As the weeks continued, tidbits of Mrs. K's colorful past and philosophy about life would somehow always creep into lectures and class discussions. We found out she had served as a volunteer nurse in a combat hospital in Japan and had "seen it all—even grown men cry." During the 1960s a wilder Mrs. K could be seen cruising the streets of San Francisco on a motorcycle, decked out in long spiked boots and short spiked hair. She later traded in her motorcycle and boots for a Fiat and white Reeboks. And there was a running joke about her age. Mrs. K could not be much less than forty-five, but just as Jack Benny was forever thirty-nine, she was forever twenty-eight. One of her T-shirts said so. Twenty-eight was a good year, she would tell us, but she never quite explained why. 9

I would come to deeply trust and respect this eccentric lady. I guess I have *Oedipus Rex* to thank for our first out-of-class meeting. We had to compose an extensive essay on the Oedipus trilogy, on which much of our semester grade would be based. Foolishly, I chose to write on the most abstract topic, predestination and divine justice. I toiled for days, torturing myself trying to come up with some definitive conclusions. Finally, I realized my struggle was merely carrying my mind farther and farther adrift in a sea of confusion. I needed someone to rescue me; I needed Mrs. K. 10

We arranged to meet in the Faculty Commons, a small, smoky room of teachers with red pens at work and administrators shooting the breeze over lunch. I crept inside with notes in hand and took a seat. She soon arrived, holding a tuna-on-wheat, a chocolate chip cookie, and the red coffeepot. "I hope you don't mind if I eat while we talk," she said, "but if you do, I'm going to eat anyway." Smile. 11

We talked the whole lunch period. I felt awkward at first, actually struggling to explain *why* I'd been struggling with the assignment. But then Mrs. K the Mentor emerged—soft-spoken, introspective, wise. I opened up to her. We sat beside each other at that table, reflecting on predestination, divine justice, and life. A ray of sunshine cut through clouds of confusion. Our reflections were interrupted by the lunch bell, but we continued later after school. Two days and two drafts later, I had gained more than just a deep understanding of *Oedipus Rex*: I had gained a friend. What was it about this woman that enabled me to reveal a different part of myself? Never before had I spoken so openly about my thoughts, or about myself. Most people did not understand my cares and thoughts. But she understood. 12

I would go back to Room 5C3 many afternoons later to sort my thoughts. To her I was Hamlet, not Erick, because of my pensive and complex nature. "Okay, Hamlet, what's on your mind?" our conversations would begin. Every writing assignment became an excuse to spend time after school talking and reflecting, with me at the wooden table and her at her stool. We digressed on everything from *Paradise Lost* to Shakespeare to "The Road Not Taken." Sometimes other students would come for help on their papers, and I would always let them go first so that I could be the last left. Often I would learn more than just literature: "Life's not black and white, it's a hazy gray, and you've always got to use that wonderful piece of machinery God gave you and question things because nothing is clear-cut." I noticed my perceptions changing, as well as my writing style. More of my character entered my writing, and the Mr. Detached Impartiality persona I once favored faded into the background. Being "creative" no longer seemed risky. She told me to put more of myself into my creations, and I listened. 13

One afternoon near the end of my senior year, I asked her about her favorite novel. "Oh, without a doubt, *Les Misérables*," she replied. "But I never could find an unedited version." On graduation day, in a sea of seniors hugging one another, red-and-blue mortarboards sailing through the air, I searched through the crowd for Mrs. K and 14 handed her a small box. Inside with a long thank-you note was a new copy of *Les Misérables*, unedited and unabridged.

I doubt that I will come across many others like Mrs. K. Only 15
she would sit with me one-on-one and review every minute detail of a draft. Only she would give up an afternoon just to shoot the breeze. Only she could I call a mentor, a confidant, and a friend. I still think of Mrs. K. Sometimes, when the pressures of college come crashing down and the order of life seems to have run amok, I go to my room, shut my eyes, sit down, and talk with Mrs. K.

"Okay, Hamlet, what's on your mind. . . ." 16

# *Big Al*

**Therron Love**

*Calhoun Community College*
*Decatur, Alabama*

I heard a loud knock on the door. Before anyone had a chance to answer, in waddled a colossal black man I had never seen before. He stood about 5'11" and weighed at least 300 pounds. His long, thick, gray-speckled black hair was covered by a black cowboy hat with a white feather sticking out of the band. His black, meticulously trimmed handlebar mustache also contained specks of gray. His round face was covered with tiny, dark razor bumps. His sagging belly rolled over the gold-plated belt buckle on his three-inch-wide leather belt. He stomped a little closer to me, wearing a friendly, mile-long grin on his pudgy face. His gap-toothed mouth held a fat, brown, foul-smelling cigar, from which he puffed thick, gray, eye-burning smoke that started to fill our living room. 1

"Come here, boy," he demanded. "Give your Uncle Al a big hug." I stood startled and unable to move. 2

"Everybody calls me Big Al," he exclaimed. "Don't be scared of me, boy. We're family." As he leaned forward to pick me up, a gigantic ash fell off his cigar and clobbered my forehead. He put his large, callus-covered hands, with their fat, stubby fingers, gently under my armpits and catapulted me toward the ceiling. Jimmy, Uncle Al's six-year-old son, stood behind him, anxiously awaiting his turn to be jettisoned upward. Uncle Al continually launched us both to within inches of the ceiling. However, for two little boys, the excitement would get even better. This was only the start of a fun-filled weekend. 3

That weekend, Big Al, Jimmy, and I enjoyed all the things that little boys loved to do. We fished, played baseball and tag, wrestled, and rode around in the back of Big Al's gold Ford pickup. Big Al seemed like a big kid to us. One afternoon, after a rowdy wrestling match out back of the house, Big Al burst into the kitchen, with 4

Jimmy and me trying hard to keep up. Covered with dust and dirt from rolling around with the two of us in the Alabama heat, Uncle Al called out for a glass of water. After several long gulps, he turned to us and grinned, "I'm ready. What are we going to do next?" He was having as much fun as we were.

Following that initial weekend, Big Al, Jimmy, and I saw each 5 other more often, and the three of us grew closer with each visit. My parents had split up when I was only three years old, and Big Al had become a surrogate father to me, and Jimmy was like a brother. Big Al treated Jimmy and me as though both of us were his sons. Whenever we traveled together, people would think that Jimmy and I were brothers because we looked so much alike; I still remember the time Big Al jokingly accused his wife, Betty, and my mother, Al's younger sister, of having had an affair with the same man because Jimmy and I resembled each other so much.

When I was thirteen years old, I won the position of starting 6 tight end on my middle school's football team. Big Al drove a hundred miles every weekend to watch me play. He also attended many of my school plays, recitals, and church choir solos (even though he did not like attending church). Big Al's huge physical presence and, more important, his support and encouragement were there for me at many of the significant events in my life.

But only three years later, the bond between Big Al, Jimmy, and 7 me changed dramatically. Jimmy started hanging out with some new friends at his high school, and Jimmy and his friends were getting into trouble. They were skipping school, stealing, fighting, vandalizing property, and using drugs. Big Al tried just about everything he could think of to correct Jimmy's delinquent behavior. He talked with him, grounded him, and even whipped him, but nothing seemed to work.

One Friday night, Jimmy and his buddies stole a car and went 8 joyriding. They were arrested and placed in a detention home. When the case went to court, Big Al convinced the judge that it would be in Jimmy's best interest if he could spend a significant amount of time in jail. The judge agreed, and he sentenced Jimmy to six months in the Tennessee State Correctional Facility for Youths. Jimmy pleaded with Big Al not to let him serve any time, but his father would not relent.

Big Al's refusal to listen to his pleas infuriated Jimmy, and he 9 deeply resented his dad's decision. Their relationship was never the same after that incident. At the time, I thought Big Al was being too hard on Jimmy, and I definitely did not want to see him incarcerated for six months. I, too, resented Big Al for what he had done to Jimmy. What I did not understand at the time was that Big Al had not done anything to Jimmy; in fact, Jimmy had done this to himself. And while Jimmy grew to hate Big Al for the decision he had made, I did not; instead, I tried to understand why Al had made that decision. I suppose Big Al was trying to help Jimmy by using tough love, but to Jimmy, it was just tough.

10 As the years passed, Big Al and I saw each other less often. I was always too busy to visit him. Going off to college, working, marrying, and raising a family occupied most of my time. Jimmy severed all ties to his father when he was eighteen years old. He was still deeply bitter about what his dad had done, and he vowed never to speak to him again. Jimmy's refusal to speak to his father hurt Big Al profoundly, but he never let it show because he knew that he had done the right thing.

11 On Thursday, March 12, 1995, at 2:18 a.m., my telephone rang. When the phone rings at that time of the morning, bad news can usually be expected. I picked up the receiver and nervously muttered, "Hello."

12 The low, somber voice on the line said, "Robert, this is your Aunt Betty. Al is in the hospital. He has lung cancer, and he wants to see you as soon as possible."

13 "I'll be there in two hours," I replied. I hung up the phone and told my wife the bad news. I leaped from the bed, quickly put on the first pair of pants I saw, threw on a shirt, grabbed shoes, and rushed out of the house barefooted. I headed for Chattanooga.

14 I arrived at Erlinger Hospital at 4:06 a.m. and rode the elevator up to the cancer floor. I walked slowly down the long, isolated corridor until I reached Uncle Al's room. Nervously, I eased the door open, trying not to disturb anyone. I was stunned at the sight of Big Al. The air rushed from my lungs, and I could hardly stand. My skin felt hot. My stomach started to churn, and I felt nauseous. Big Al did not resemble the person I had known for most of my life.

15 The radiation and chemotherapy treatments had robbed Big Al of both his long, thick hair and his luxurious handlebar mustache. He had also lost nearly 200 pounds. He no longer had an appetite because of the cancer treatments. The little food that he did manage to eat he would vomit. His dull brown skin drooped loosely, and his face appeared to be sinking past his cheekbones. His eyes looked yellowish with large, dilated pupils. Big Al was waiting for death.

A white sheet and a powder blue blanket were neatly tucked below his chest. An array of colorful flowers and get-well cards lined the windowsill. A food tray had been pushed against the wall. On a chair in the corner sat his black cowboy hat with its white feather. 16

"Where is Jimmy?" Big Al gasped, as he gradually focused his eyes on me. 17

"I don't know, Uncle Al," I responded. "I was hoping he'd be here. How are you feeling?" I asked reluctantly. 18

"Not too good. I'm dying," he replied in a soft, faint voice. "The doctors say I've only got a few hours to live. Where is Jimmy?" he asked again. 19

Sadly, I did not have an answer for him. Betty whispered to me that she had begged and pleaded with Jimmy to come to the hospital, but he had refused. After all these years, Jimmy still harbored hateful feelings toward him. Big Al's dying apparently meant nothing to Jimmy. 20

When I was a child growing up without a father in my life, Big Al had become my surrogate father. Now, as he lay dying without his only son by his side, I was determined to be his surrogate son. I reached over and took my father's hand. We sat quietly for a while. Big Al's breathing gradually became softer and shallower. After a while, he closed his eyes, took one last gasp of air, and died peacefully. 21

# *The Eyes in the Mirror*

**Angel Nguyen**
*University of Houston*
*Houston, Texas*

As soon as I walked into the house I was overwhelmed by the luscious smell of an array of spices. The fragrance of lemon, red and green pepper, and catfish floated through the air, taking every room hostage. The overwhelming aroma could only mean one thing: Grandma was here. My suspicion was confirmed at the sound of her melancholy voice singing her usual song of death and war. Despite her tiny figure, she possessed a strong voice that penetrated throughout the quiet house, "Why do we have to fight, why do our people have to die? God, please help me, help me be strong." She sang in a Northern Vietnamese dialect; I understood the song only because I had heard it time and time again. Like a bird, she was always singing, and the songs were always the same: songs of love and loss, life and death, and pain and suffering. I rolled my eyes as she began another song about the hardships of a young girl picking sugarcane in the field. Her slim upper lip would make a peculiar curve at the high notes, and I could not help but secretly laugh just thinking about it. 1

Many years would pass before I could fully understand the importance of those songs. They were the story of her life, thus a part of my life. An intense flame ignited in her eyes as she emphasized each and every note. The songs came from deep within her soul. Although she knew a total of only five or six songs, she had the ability to invent a new story just by changing her tone of voice. 2

Suddenly, Grandma stopped singing and called out, "Angel? Did you just come in, little one?" Quickly, I inspected my appearance. My best pink Sunday dress was covered with dirt and grass stains from chasing a frog just a moment ago. Small twigs and leaves poked out of my hair and the cute braids my mom made were now in tangles. Grandma would kill me if she saw me like this. The bathroom was only a few feet away from the front door where I was standing. 3

The only problem was I had to pass by the kitchen. I took in a deep breath and ran. Just as I came to the kitchen I closed my eyes, rationalizing that if I could not see Grandma, she too could not see me. I rushed to get cleaned up, looking over my shoulder every other second just in case of a surprise attack, though she never came.

Precisely at 6:30 p.m. Grandma yelled, "Time for dinner!" I sullenly dragged myself from the living room to the dining room before she had the chance to yell at me for watching too much television. Sitting at the head of the table was Grandma in one of her many traditional Vietnamese dresses made from delicate black and white silk. The thin, soft cloth covered her long, skinny arms and neck and perfectly hugged her tiny waist. Long slits on both sides of the dress rose to her hips, exposing common black slacks underneath. Her boyish, short white hair glistened in the dining room's light. As I sat down at the end of the table, I could feel her eyes carefully watching me as if she were trying to see through me. There was something in her deep brown eyes that made me believe she could see into my heart and soul, a belief founded on an incident that had occurred several years earlier. 4

I once broke my mother's expensive vase, and because no one saw me I believed I could glue it together and no one would be the wiser. A few days later, when my mother attempted to put roses into the vase, it shattered. Both my mother and Grandma questioned me about it, and, without hesitation, I lied. My mother readily accepted my avowal of innocence, but my Grandma gave me *the look*. I always thought she had eyes in the back of her head: she watched and knew everything but never said anything. She refrained from directly scolding me or verbally expressing herself to me, but the look was enough to unnerve and frighten me. She was a silent assassin who preferred to force me into submission through her icy stares. Her techniques were subtle yet extremely deliberate and masterfully effective. She squinted her eyes and stared into me, causing me to look away. A disapproving frown formed on her slightly parted lips, as though she wanted to say something but was too upset to do so. I could feel my shame and her disappointment, and both haunted me as I tossed and turned in my bed until I surrendered and confessed the next morning. 5

I stayed quiet throughout dinner and started to pick at my food, taking out the vegetables and herbs, unknowingly setting myself up for another attack. "You know, Thi," my Grandma started to say to my mom in a very serious tone, "you should really teach your daughter some manners. It's not proper for a young girl to play 6 in mud." I hated when Grandma talked about me as if I were not there.

"Grandma!" I protested. She ignored me. 7

"Why isn't she eating that?" she asked, pointing to my untouched bowl of soup. 8

"I don't like it," I said softly, almost afraid of the consequences of my answer, even though the question was not directed at me. 9

Just as I feared, she was furious. "That's ridiculous! She's Vietnamese; she has to eat it. She isn't leaving this table until she does." 10

I glanced at my mom for help, but she shook her head, indicating I had to listen. 11

Five months later, I was forced to pack all my belongings and move into my sister's room. Grandma was moving in for an indefinite stay. Angry over having to move, I made it my mission to stay away from her for the most part, but at the same time I found her mysteriously fascinating. Still afraid of her, I watched her from afar. I watched her as she walked off in her thin black sandals to church, ten blocks away, every morning at sunrise to pray. Then at night, she would sit silently on the porch and pray under the stars. "If you have God in your life you need nothing else," she would always say with a suggestive smile, revealing a chipped tooth in the corner of her mouth from a bicycle accident in Vietnam. While my parents were working, my Grandma took care of all the daily house chores and looked after my sister and me. Despite the fact that she was well into her eighties, she had an unbelievable strength when she put her heart and soul into her work. Yet she was the same woman who could only eat rice soup because her stomach was not strong enough to hold solids. She never once complained about the laundry load being too heavy or there being too many dirty dishes to wash. She did everything with a smile and a song. 12

The only time I let myself get close to her was when I assisted her with the preparation of dinner. I would sit on the kitchen counter as she skillfully rolled dumplings into perfect little swans and listen to her talk about Chinese philosophy. She knew everything there was to know about Confucius, Chuang Tzu, and Daoism. Watching her cut vegetables, I was always amazed at how rough and hard her hands looked, yet her touch was always gentle and soft. She also had a way of carrying herself with unbelievable grace. During our evenings in the kitchen, I learned that she sought to live life to the fullest even when life seemed cruel. Life's cruelties could be seen when she wore a sleeveless shirt in the summer, for it was then 13

I could see a fairly large bullet wound in her right arm. I knew my looking at it hurt her. I knew my asking her about it hurt her even more, but she would simply smile and say, "Little Angel, you must always remember that life will always have its wars, but war will never take away life's beauty."

Within a few years Grandma's songs slowly became more and more faint until they were only a quiet whisper. She did not sing anymore, opting instead for utter stillness and silence. "I'm so tired," she would say. I just had to believe she was just too tired. Grandma was a tiny elderly woman whose body could not keep up with her any longer. At the age of 96, my Grandma ceased to sing forever. 14

The importance of my Grandma's presence in my life did not emerge until after she was gone. She was my connection to my past, my culture, and my ancestors. By knowing who she was and what she stood for, I know a little more of myself. Ten years have passed since she died, and as I look at her picture, the eyes that I was once so afraid of seem different to me now. I have finally learned to see through their sternness, and I have found a flood of emotions and warmth behind them. When I look into the mirror, I see her eyes staring back at me. 15

# 4 *Writing Profiles*

When a piece of writing has immediacy, readers become transfixed. When a profile has immediacy, the event, person, or place seems to unfold before our eyes in part because the author has identified what is unique about the subject, and this distinctive quality draws us into the text. Yet, for a profile to succeed, it needs to do more than merely identify what is distinctive about the topic. Profile writers must also describe, often in vivid detail. In this respect a profile writer resembles a reporter on a television news program: on the scene to capture the intensity and detail of the moment. Additionally, profile writers, keenly aware of their readers, are conscientious about when and where they introduce their information, often using description, observation, and dialogue to communicate their information gradually, methodically building a complete picture of the subject. As you read the essays in this chapter, notice how each explores and presents the lesser known, the unpredictable, the surprising.

In "Our Daily Bread," Linda Kampel profiles a soup kitchen that would seem to present nothing out of the ordinary. Yet, as Kampel states in her opening, walking into this place "is like stepping into a different world." Alternating between descriptions of setting and people to blend effectively the unfamiliar and the familiar, Kampel keeps readers interested by presenting surprising new information while simultaneously letting readers feel connected to the people who are so crucial to her subject. Kampel also effectively weaves her own observations and responses with the quotations she's gathered from her interviews with others. This blend of the personal and factual enable her to narrow the distance between herself and her subject; subsequently, that distance is narrowed for readers as well.

We have all probably wondered what goes on when the supermarket locks its doors for the night. In "True Worker," Erik Epple invites his audience into the back rooms of a grocery store as well as introduces the individuals who work during the dead of night. Profiling the night shift's crew chief, Larry Hershman, Epple, both by showing and telling, deftly contrasts the attitudes and work ethics of Larry with the younger crew members. While the essay seemingly sets out to confirm or deny Larry's mythological status among the grocery store employees, Epple's conclusion not only discovers an alternative answer but tacitly asks the reader, "What kind of worker are you?"

Sarah Sucher knows her views of midwives and their profession are stereotypical and based on ignorance. Her search to broaden her own understanding, in "No Nuns Here," leads Sucher to the Woman's Care and Midwifery Center, where she meets Pam Yach. Remaining open-minded, Sucher balances her expectations against the reality of who and what midwives are to construct a profile not only of an individual midwife but of a profession. Using description, dialogue, and observation, Sucher portrays a profession far removed from the stereotypical view of "dour-looking wom[e]n scurrying around looking for towels and blankets."

The sometimes poetic style of Brenda Crow's "The Dance with Glass" enables readers to better understand the relationship between one's profession and one's art. Crow's visit to Dan Daggett's glass studio is, on the one hand, a detailed descriptive essay. Yet, on the other hand, Crow's style reflects, in part, the actions the glassblower performs in creating his art. Between Crow's precise depiction of Daggett's studio and the materials, equipment, and glassware that occupy it and her rhythmical explanation of the process by which Daggett creates, readers are afforded an insightful view of a man who is working at a vanishing art.

A person's avocation can sometimes become his or her consuming passion, as Glenda Sourisseau illustrates in "Homemade Horror." Sourisseau's profile of Glenn Keihl and his love affair with fear introduces readers to a man who has turned a simple, neighborly competition into an elaborate maze of horror and mayhem. In presenting Keihl to her readers, Sourisseau details the creativity and ingenuity Keihl has used in creating Glenn's Gory Garage Haunt and catalogues the abnormal creatures that have sprung from Keihl's workshop. Yet ultimately readers are able to picture not a person who is obsessed with terror and dread and carnage but a man who simply and truly enjoys his pastime and merely wants others to have the opportunity to share in that enjoyment.

# *Our Daily Bread*

**Linda Kampel**

*Pennsylvania State University, York*
*York, Pennsylvania*

To anyone who has the luxury of regular meals and a safe place to call home, walking through the entrance of Our Daily Bread soup kitchen is like stepping into a different world. Our Daily Bread operates out of a two-room cinder-block building in York, Pennsylvania, that has been transformed into a kitchen and dining area where nearly three hundred poverty-stricken people come every day to eat. The front doors open at 10 a.m., and the first thing you notice when they do is a large room with rows of six-foot metal tables, dim lights that cast gray shadows, and walls that are painted in 1970s "harvest gold," which has dulled with time. 1

In the back of the room there is a stainless-steel, cafeteria-style serving counter where about thirty-five people are being served hot coffee and donuts. As gloomy as the surroundings may sound, the majority of the people in the place seem to be comfortably familiar with the daily routine of standing in line waiting for lunch to be served. Occasionally, someone tells a joke or a funny story and one or more people laugh, making the atmosphere seem almost cheery. 2

As I'm observing the moment, a tall, heavyset black man wearing a dark cap suddenly starts yelling at an invisible companion who has obviously upset him. "F--- you! I'll do what I want!" he yells. Everyone else in the room goes on with their business. "I said I'm going to do what I want. Just leave me alone!" 3

At first, it seems like this man could be a real threat, but when I ask him what his name is, he very calmly says, "My name's Andy." 4

There is something sad about the look in Andy's eyes, and within a few minutes, he's arguing again with whomever it is that has made him so unhappy. I find it hard to keep from getting involved and wanting to find Andy the help that he obviously seems to need for his problems. It's hard not to feel his pain. 5

At 11 a.m., the crowd grows to about 80 people, and volunteers are preparing to serve lunch. By 11:30, the number increases to 120, and by 12:15, there are close to 250 men and women, and a handful of children, making their way into the line that moves like a well-rehearsed act in a play. Today's meal consists of vegetable soup, broccoli, bread, and tuna-noodle casserole, with a choice of either lemonade or coffee to drink. People of every age, gender, and race move through the line. No one is turned away. 6

Carol, a thirty-five-year-old black woman dressed in clean but worn-out clothes, says that she has been coming here for about two years. "Most people who come here aren't homeless," she says. "We all have a place to live and all. It's just that sometimes meals are a problem. Some people come here because it's a social thing, you know. You take a break from whatever you're doing. You come in here and have some food and talk to people you know." 7

A tall white man, about sixty-five years of age and dressed in dirty old clothes, walks past us. He has donut powder all over his mouth and chin. "That's so sad," Carol says. "He doesn't even know it's there. That poor man. Now *he* needs help. At least he's here in a place where he'll be taken care of." 8

At first it's easy to think that Carol's problems aren't all that bad, perhaps because she has become so good at convincing herself that this way of life is normal. You fall right into her train of thought. But later, thinking back, you can't help realizing that the majority of the people who come to Our Daily Bread do need help of some kind or they wouldn't be there. They're either so lost that they can't find themselves anymore or have accepted this daily routine as the reality of a bad hand they've been dealt in life. 9

Around 12:30 p.m., a volunteer worker walks over to a microphone at the end of the serving counter and asks, "Has everyone gotten the food they need to eat?" No one says a word. "If anyone needs more to eat, please come up and get as much as you want." 10

A few people return to the counter for second helpings, but most people are beginning to leave. They've been well fed and maybe somehow given the boost they need to make it through the day. 11

At the helm of this well-run operation are two people, Joe McCormick and Marie Rohleder, both of whom have a genuine and unconditional interest in making sure that for at least two and a half hours a day, anyone who needs a hot meal or emotional support in a warm, dry place can find it within these walls. 12

Joe McCormick, the business manager, is a tall, white-haired, sixty-year-old man whose smile lets you know right away that he is a very special human being, the "real thing." Joe cares about every inch of this place and about the people who come here for help. Joe is semi-retired now, but he still takes care of all the expenses of Our Daily Bread, keeps track of the donations, and sends out thank-you notes to all those who contribute food or services. Every Monday, Joe is in charge of food preparation and serving. 13

"We've been here for seven years now," he says. "We're open Monday through Friday from 10 a.m. to 12:30 p.m. You should have seen the place we were in before we moved here. It was hell on earth, in the basement of Cristo Salvador, a local Spanish church. The kitchen was about a third of the size of this one here. There was barely enough room for a dishwasher and a stove. That place used to get about 150 degrees in the summertime when we were making food, and there were times when the water on the floor from rainstorms was six inches deep. We were afraid to use anything electric." Joe lights a cigarette. "Back then we were serving about 107 people a day. Now we're serving around 300. It used to be 400 before September House started its senior citizen outreach program, but I'll let Marie tell you about that later." 14

Cartons of pastries arrive through the back door, so Joe goes over to help bring them in. When he returns, he leans against a stack of crates. 15

"Last Thanksgiving we were really sweating it out because we supply Helping Hands with their turkeys, and we hardly had any turkeys at all. Then right after the holidays, we got a call to come and pick up fifty of them. It's feast or famine around here. When Chuck E. Cheese closed down last year, I got two truckloads of pizzas and birthday cakes. Boy, were they good. People still come in here and ask, 'Do you have any more of those birthday cakes?' We're never at a loss for resources for food, it seems. It's not always the greatest, but it's out there. York County is a very giving place." 16

Joe tells me, "Just a second," and when he returns, he is with a dark-haired woman about thirty-five years of age, wearing a blue nylon jacket. She has the same welcoming smile that Joe has, and I can't help thinking how lucky everyone here is to have these two people on their side. Joe introduces the woman as Marie, who is, by her own definition, the inventory-control specialist. 17

"In other words, I make sure that all the food gets put in the freezer, which explains the jacket. I also rotate the food on the shelves so that nothing stays around too long." 18

Marie also takes on the responsibilities of food preparation and serving on Thursdays and Fridays. 19

"There's a guy named Charlie who takes care of Tuesdays and Wednesdays, but he's not here right now. Anyway, an organization called September House started an outreach program a couple of years ago. They go and pick up our senior citizens and take them for meals at their senior citizen center. They're much better off over there because they get the attention they really need. That's why the number of people we serve here has dropped off slightly. It's a wonderful organization. It's hard not to get involved sometimes. There are some people you can't help but get involved with. They need that. And there are some people who come and go. We just found out today that one fellow we get involved with *a lot* just got sent to jail last night. Busted for drugs. It's heartbreaking sometimes because you know how hard they've been trying. There was one guy who used to do dishes for us. Lester. He tried *so* hard to stay sober, and he just couldn't do it. Eventually he died from alcohol poisoning." 20

"That's the hardest kind," Joe says. "You see these people and you know that no matter what the hell they do, they're in a hole. And they're never gonna get out." 21

One of the volunteers comes over and asks where to put a tray filled with pumpkin bread. 22

"That's Pat," Marie says after she points her toward a storage shelf. "She's one of our regular volunteers. She comes in almost every day, along with the volunteers from at least one church group. We get about fifty volunteers a week. The only problem is that no one wants to clean up—everyone wants to serve or cook, but as soon as 12:30 hits, *boom*, they're out the door. York College is sending over a group of students this Saturday to paint these walls. And the group Up with People is coming in tomorrow, I think, to help out. I'm glad they're coming because Fridays are the worst. For some reason that's the day when the people who really are in desperate need come in, so that they can load up for the weekend. We always have extra bread, so we can give out a couple of loaves to everyone." 23

When 12:45 arrives, the volunteers are finished serving lunch. There is clean-up work to be done, and Joe and Marie take their place among the volunteers so that they will soon be able to call it a day. As I start to leave, it is hard to know how to feel. On one hand, it's really sad to see people trying to survive without the daily things that most of us take for granted. On the other hand, until it isn't 24 necessary for people to have to worry about where their next meal will come from, it's comforting to know that wonderful people like Joe and Marie at places like Our Daily Bread are out there doing their best to ease some of the burden.

# *True Worker*

**Erik Epple**

*Bowling Green State University*
*Bowling Green, Ohio*

I've been working at Kroger's Supermarket in Springville, Ohio, for two weeks now, and my coworkers keep mentioning Larry Harshman, head of the store's grocery department. Depending on whom I talk to, Larry is either the most solitary, antisocial person on staff, or he's some kind of mythic hero, like Paul Bunyan or Pecos Bill. 1

I decide I wanted to meet Larry for myself. The mystique around him only grows when I learn he works the graveyard shift. I head back to the supermarket at 11:00 one Thursday night and introduce myself to Larry. As we talk, I begin to realize that Larry Harshman is a far more complicated person than my coworkers would have me believe. 2

The chattering of mechanical devices, the smashing of falling crates, and the ripping of cardboard would cause most people to cover their ears. Larry welcomes the noises, though. They prove to him that he is working hard and also ease his loneliness. 3

Sitting across from Larry in the dimly lit break room, I am inspired by his work ethic. Over twenty-seven years, Larry has worked his way up from a bagger to head of the grocery department. Clark Carr, the store manager, has nothing but praise for Larry: "He is a very reliable worker, one that I go to every time I need something done." 4

Larry, however, is beginning to feel his age: "It's my back; I just can't move as quick anymore." 5

However, other Kroger employees believe that no one there can outwork Larry, despite his fifty-year-old body. Whether he is cutting open boxes or unloading a truck, he seems to defy his limitations and works in a flurry of activity, in an environment of ordered chaos. *Efficient, practiced*, and *precise* are words that best describe Larry. 6

Larry's days are exact: arise, go to work, return home, sleep. The routine is periodically interrupted when he goes out to eat with a 7 friend, but such interruptions are rare. And while Larry works nine to five, he does not go to work in the morning, like most other Americans, because his workday begins at nine p.m.

"I've never been much of a social person," Larry states with downcast eyes. "That's why I work third shift." Larry prefers to work alone and would rather have just one good friend than many. He likes those nights when only he and Carol—a night cashier and close friend of his—work the shelves. His obsession with work and desire for solitude have destroyed his home life. His wife of twenty-five years filed for divorce, leaving Larry totally dispirited. 8

"I like being alone," he comments, "but alone doesn't mean without anyone to care about you. She was always that one special person in my life and was always there when I needed someone to listen to me. Now she is gone, and all that I have left are my friends at Kroger." 9

After a moment's quiet, I ask Larry to explain his job. He sips his Pepsi and responds: "After my break, I'll show you." 10

Fifteen minutes later, he hauls himself out of the metal chair and nods toward the door. Following him into the back room, I am surprised by his change of mood. His eyes narrow, and cursing under his breath, he falls into step with another employee as they survey the work left undone by the day crew. 11

"Looks like another long night for us, Oscar," Larry proclaims to his companion, cursing again. 12

"Just once," Oscar growls, "I'd like to see those lazy bastards work a night shift." 13

Grabbing the handle of a pallet jack—a large machine that resembles a miniature forklift—and rolling the jack toward him, Larry begins speaking to me over his shoulder. 14

"First, we unload the truck, which usually isn't too bad, but can be a pain in the ass at times," he declares, as the twin prongs on the jack slide under the first pallet of groceries. 15

I watch Larry repeatedly maneuver the forklift in and out of the semi's trailer, each time appearing with another pallet full of boxes; within a half-hour the sixty-foot trailer is empty. When all of the pallets are lined along the back wall, Larry pulls a box cutter out of his rear pocket. 16

I watch as Larry mechanically slits the tops, one by one, off of each box. Although working at a frenetic pace, he never cuts into the groceries inside. After removing each top, he places the open boxes on cart-like devices called wheelers. Four workers appear from the 17 front of the store to take the now-filled wheelers inside. As the night continues, I discover Larry always has a wheeler filled before someone comes back for a new one.

Everyone agrees Larry is the key to a successful night. 18

"It worries me sometimes, watching him gimp around the break 19
room, but his age never shows through his work," comments Rita, an employee who works the wheelers.

"He gets six weeks out of every year for vacation. During those 20
weeks, Oscar loads up the wheelers and Spencer unloads the truck, and everything just goes to hell," complains Mark, another worker.

Returning the box cutter to his pocket, Larry calls break over the 21
loudspeaker. As everyone else begins shuffling toward the break room for a few smokes or a snack, Larry heads for the front of the store, buys himself a can of soda, then sits down on one of the register belts.

"It's just not like it used to be around here," Larry mumbles. 22
"Clark takes away all of our help, and the ones who *are* working don't take it seriously. It's all a big joke these days. Some of the workers spend most of their time on the clock talking on the telephone to God only knows who. Others just joke around and never go beyond what is expected of them. The spirit of working and earning your pay is gone. That gets to me sometimes."

Glancing around me, I see exactly what Larry means. Empty 23
boxes are scattered up and down the aisles, left on the floor for the morning crew to pick up. The six workers unloading the wheelers inside the store cannot keep up with Larry, the only person working in the back on the dock. Not only are wheelers spread around the store, still loaded, but many more are choking the back; I weave my way through a narrow canyon of wheelers to reach the break room.

"He just takes his job too seriously. He needs to lighten up, 24
enjoy himself," remarks a cocky, tall worker, whom I later find out is Greg. "If you want my opinion," he continues, "he needs a woman."

As if to add gloom to the picture of Larry's personal life, Rita 25
chimes in: "Oh, you know old Larry will never get himself another woman; he doesn't even know how to act around one anymore."

The crew falls into its own private thoughts. Through the 26
canyon of wheelers, I can see Larry still sitting by himself in the front. Half an hour later, everyone is back at work.

"No reason to keep stacking up the wheelers," Larry growls, as 27
he stares at the many wheelers waiting to be taken into the store and unloaded. "They'll just get so backed up that no one can get into the back."

Larry turns and begins stacking the now empty pallets and cleaning up the docking area. When he is satisfied that everything is in order, he takes the remaining wheelers out to the front. Instead of leaving the work to the other employees, Larry begins to help them stock the shelves. With Larry helping, the others finish in less than an hour. 28

"Now is when I slack because all the work is done," Larry states. "There is nothing left to do, even if anyone wanted to. It makes no sense to slack before the work is over." 29

Driving away that night, I realized that Larry Harshman was neither mythic hero nor recluse but someone who represented a time when how well a person performed his job was a measure of that person's worth. It is an attitude that his coworkers, both those who see him as Superman and those who don't, do not perceive or understand. But in just one night, I learned not only to appreciate him as a hard worker but also to respect him as someone who refuses to let unenthusiastic coworkers or his own physical decline stand in the way of getting the job done. 30

# *No Nuns Here*

**Sarah Sucher**

*Des Moines Area Community College*
*Ankeny, Iowa*

Throughout human history, babies have been entering the world with the assistance of midwives. Historians have discovered references to midwifery, the practice of midwives, in Egyptian papyri and ancient Hindu documents; midwifery was a respected occupation during Greek and Roman times and continued to be widely practiced through the European Middle Ages ("History"). In what would become the United States of America, "Native Americans had midwives within their various tribes," while "[m]idwifery in Colonial America began as an extension of European practices" ("Midwifery"). As an active participant in the birthing process, midwives are part of the excitement and joy accompanying a child's birth, offering education, medical supervision, and care for the new mother and child. And although the use of midwives has waned over the past one hundred or so years, expectant parents are, once again, turning to midwives to assist in the delivery of their children. 1

Until I began to research midwifery, I was ignorant of the subject. To me, midwives were overweight nuns. The word *midwife*[1] alone made me think of a dour-looking woman scurrying around looking for towels and blankets. I pictured cold, empty hallways, with crucifixes hanging on every wall. I envisioned a small bed, made up neatly in white linens, pressed up against the wall of a tiny room. No colors, no sounds—just the nuns and the anxiously waiting mother. After my visit with Pam Yach, a practicing midwife, I realized my ideas about midwives were completely wrong. 2

As I entered the Women's Care and Midwifery Center, I found myself in what looked like my doctor's office. The walls were adorned with pastel floral pictures, some with birds, but no crucifixes. I sat in a small waiting room with only five chairs and a tiny table. The table was stacked high with old issues of *Vogue, Seventeen,* 3

*People,* and *Newsweek,* not what I thought the reading material would be at a midwifery office. The environment was noisy and colorful, not quiet and bare. Telephone operators announced over loudspeakers phone lines that needed answering, and medical assistants were busy discussing patients' files and charts. Gray and lavender walls were lined with large bulletin boards advertising the month's latest medical/midwifery news. Posters and decorations hung from every door in the office, and Valentine's Day hearts hung from the ceiling. This was not the dull, dry environment I expected, and so far, I hadn't seen anyone who remotely resembled a nun. I was beginning to wonder if I was in the right office.

"Are you Sarah?" a soft voice asked. I looked up; a short, petite, 4
blond-haired woman extended her hand. "I am Pam Yach." I shook her hand, introduced myself, and followed her back to her office.

"She can't be a midwife," I thought, surprised by her appear- 5
ance. "She isn't fat; she probably doesn't even weigh a hundred pounds." Moreover, Pam was wearing khakis, a denim shirt, and brown boots. And her ears were double pierced. We arrived at her office and immediately her phone rang.

"Excuse me a minute, Sarah," she said, picking up the receiver. 6
"Yes, Karen Booker called last night, and she wants to come in now. She said her water broke. I told her to come in if she thought she was ready to deliver. Okay, I'll call her." As she talked, she reached for a handful of neon-colored Tiny Tarts. She later explained that they were her daily pick-me-up.

Pam, as a midwife, is responsible for the care and education of the 7
expectant mother up until birth and the postnatal care of mother and child following the delivery. Pam explained, "Midwifery is not just delivering a baby and leaving. It is a full process from beginning to end. It is an event that requires lots of family and personal planning and also a lot of care. That is what midwives are here to help the mothers do."

The philosophy that midwives have toward childbirth is quite 8
different from that of physicians and obstetricians. According to Pam, childbirth is a normal and natural process of life. Doctors, she feels, instead of just being patient and letting the birth take its natural course, are too quick to intervene and to try and hurry the process along. Pam believes that too many doctors see the birthing process as a medical procedure they are performing, not a mother's life event that they are assisting in.

Pam is a certified nurse-midwife (CNM) and an advanced regis- 9
tered nurse practitioner (ARNP).[2] I asked Pam the difference

between her title and a doctor's. "A few thousand dollars!" she responded. "But seriously . . . doctors are trained in the medical field more extensively than midwives. Doctors are required to attend four years of medical school, and midwives are not. Also, doctors have extremely long residency requirements, and ours is somewhere around six weeks, depending on the training program you are a part of." Pam explained that like doctors, midwives are licensed to perform all of the same tests a woman needs throughout her pregnancy. Many times, midwives can provide these services at a much lower cost than doctors. "The fact that the costs are lower in a low-risk, normal pregnancy is just one of the reasons that many women and families are starting to use midwife services, especially considering how expensive having a baby is nowadays," Pam commented.

Pam, Patty Blue—another midwife in the office—and I dis- 10
cussed some of the preconceptions that people have of midwives. Pam jokingly said, "Yeah, we aren't a bunch of lesbians like everyone thinks we are, and we don't offer herbs for our patients to smoke before they give birth."

Patty chimed in, "And I'm not fat. Everyone always assumes that 11
midwives are fat."

Both Pam and Patty admit they understand why people think the 12
way they do about midwives because the reality has seldom been portrayed. "When was the last time you saw a young, skinny, big-boobed midwife on *ER*?" exclaimed Patty. "You don't."

Pam and Patty hope to make people more aware of the Women's 13
Care and Midwifery Center in an effort to better educate others on the role of midwives. "Midwifing is actually very popular because the costs are less, sometimes far less, than what one would pay for a hospital birth," said Pam. "Hospitals are getting so crowded in the bigger cities that patients are looking for a more personal, hands-on relationship with the staff involved in their child's birth. That's when they call a midwife. That type of one-on-one service is 100 percent guaranteed."

At lunch, I asked Pam what it is about her job that keeps her 14
spirits so high and the office atmosphere so light. She smiled at me and said, "Well, I would have to say the reward of doing something important and getting credit for it. Nothing is worse than being in delivery for three hours and having the doctor come in for the last ten minutes to steal the show, just for pulling the baby out of the woman. That always torqued me. The nurses and technicians are overlooked, and the doctor is the hero of the moment. If it were not

for the assistants, the doctor might face a number of complications. Also, I wanted to help moms prepare for their new baby and teach them how to take care of the newborn once it arrived. Knowing that I played a part somewhere in a child's life really makes a difference to me."

15 Before I left Pam's office that afternoon, I confessed to my previous view of midwives and told her I was surprised by my discoveries and at how different midwifery is from what I thought it would be. I left the Women's Care and Midwifery Center with not only a better understanding of midwifery services but a new appreciation for the women who are committed to reviving the personal relationship that once existed between patients and practitioners.

## NOTES

1. The term *midwife* derives from the Old English word *midwif,* which translates as "with woman."

2. For the definitions of the several types of midwives, see <http://motherstuff.com/html/2midwifery-types.html>.

## WORKS CITED

"History of Midwifery." 19 July 2000. Parkland School of Nurse Midwifery. 17 Feb. 2003 <http://www3.utsouthwestern.edu/parkland/midwifery/mdwfhistory.html>.

"Midwifery in the United States." 31 Dec. 1999. Parkland School of Nurse Midwifery. 17 Feb. 2003 <http://www3.utsouthwestern.edu/parkland/midwifery/mdwfhsus.html>.

# *The Dance with Glass*

**Brenda Crow**

*Front Range Community College, Larimer*

*Fort Collins, Colorado*

The door to one of the ovens is opened. Inside the light is intensely bright, glowing brighter than a volcano's lava. Four feet away, it feels as though going any closer would surely melt flesh from bone. Clear glass is being heated to a Day-Glo bright 2,150 degrees Fahrenheit. 1

The glassblower pushes one end of a five-foot-long stainless steel rod, called a *punty,* a couple of inches deep into the molten glass. He picks up the lump of molten glass and twirls the rod continuously as he closes the door of the oven and moves over to a metal worktable. He then lays the punty on to the tabletop and begins rolling the molten glass along the table's surface. "This is *mavering,*" he tells me. 2

On the right side of the table he has laid out three rows, each five inches long and a half-inch wide, of tiny, colored glass chips, poured from a collection of clear plastic bags and an odd assortment of coffee cans and Styrofoam cups that surround the table's edge. "*Frit,*" he says. 3

From oven, to table, to *glory hole,* a kiln-like oven with no door, the glassblower moves the molten glass. Glowing. Hot, hot, hot. The glassblower lays the punty on a small metal stand with two small rollers on the top. The opposite end of the punty is in the glory hole, reheating the glass. 4

"*Glory hole* got its name because that's where all the glory happens. That's where all the colors come together," he says. 5

The glassblower is constantly turning, always turning, and moving, always moving the punty inside the glory hole. Right to left, left to right. "*Flashing,*" he says. 6

Back to the table, more mavering. He then lays the liquid glass, which is suspended on the end of the punty, into the frit. He then lifts the punty, rotates it a half turn, and again lays the liquid glass into the frit. He repeats the process yet again. He works quickly, the 7 punty always moving, always spinning. Back to the glory hole, reheating the glass and melting the frit into the core of clear, molten glass. More mavering, again to the glory hole. Spinning, turning, spinning, rotating.

Quickly he lays the edge of the punty on one of the metal brackets, pushes it forward into the glory hole, slides in behind it, and sits with his back toward me. The pressed-wood bench he sits on sags slightly from his weight. He pulls the punty back, bringing the end with the molten glass closer to him. In swift, fluid movements, he lifts a wet, wooden block from one of the murky, water-filled, five-gallon buckets on either side of the bench. The blackened cup-shaped block on a long wooden handle has a section of the side cut away. With the punty resting on the bracket, he touches the glass with the cup-shaped block, steam rises, water hisses. He rounds the molten glass with it. 8

Up, off the bench, moving always moving, glory hole, more flashing, spinning, more spinning, back to the bench in fluid movement, this is the dance with glass. He lifts a pair of shears, places them an inch from the far end of the glass, and applies pressure. Turning, always turning the punty, slower now, pulling with the shears, extending the softened glass and causing a swirl pattern to form from the frit he had embedded into the clear glass moments earlier. Waiting now, gauging the temperature of the glass, he squeezes the shears harder, then pinches off a round piece of glass the size of a baseball. "Christmas ornament," states the glassblower. 9

A sign, in royal blue letters four feet by two feet on a white background to the left of the door on the old brick wall, reads, "Daggett Glass Studio—Hand Blown Art Glass." The studio is housed in an old, nondescript building in downtown Loveland, Colorado. The studio is somewhat cluttered, but a couple hundred beautiful and delicate pieces of blown and hand-shaped glass line the wall on my right. Some pieces are hanging from strands of nearly invisible fishing line; others sit on cloth-covered tables and display cases. The glass is in every shade of green, blue, red, purple, orange, and yellow and in every conceivable shape I can imagine. Vases; bowls; paperweights; perfume bottles; candy dishes; "witch balls," which, when hung in a window, are supposed to keep evil spirits at bay; Christmas ornaments; icicles; candy canes; fruit; and fish are on display. As are solid, dome-shaped pieces of clear glass with mother-of-pearl powder suspended in them, pieces the glassblower calls "Ice Fog," which he created one day as he was "playing." 10

The studio has one exposed brick wall, on which the glass is displayed. The other walls are paneled on the bottom one-third of the wall and painted white on the upper two-thirds. The ceiling is covered with old Victorian pressed tin tiles that have been painted a rust color. The floor is old and wooden, worn from the passage of many years and many feet. Heavy sheets of metal, which squeak when walked on and are joined together with what appears to be scuffed-up duct tape, cover the floor between the ovens and the worktables. The back of the studio is four-feet deep in clutter; I imagine only the owner knows what resides there. To my left are the ovens. The annealing oven is at 950 degrees. It holds finished pieces of glass and is set to cool at 60 degrees per hour in order to limit stress on the cooling glass. Glass cooled too quickly shatters. Beyond the annealing oven is the oven that holds the molten glass. Between the two, glowing bright yellow-orange, is the glory hole. Discarded pieces of worked glass line the floor under the annealing oven. Covered in dust that only partially obscures their beauty, they look like discarded jewels. 11

As I draw nearer, the man sitting behind the desk at the far end of the studio bounds out of his chair and strides toward me as he says hello. Dan Daggett is a tall, rotund man with a warm, friendly demeanor. He has pleasant brown eyes; curly, somewhat frizzy, brownish-gray hair, which he often runs his fingers through; and a graying mustache, which completely covers his upper lip. He is casually dressed in an untucked white T-shirt, khakis, and tennis shoes. I feel immediately comfortable in his studio and begin asking questions and commenting on the wonderful pieces of art glass he has created. Dan holds up one of his many multicolored, iridescent swirled glass icicles: "A woman from a magazine called me and asked if I would mind if they featured these in an article of fun things to buy. Would I *mind*? I would be delighted," he smiles. 12

From the glory hole, Dan grabs a *blowpipe*, a hollow punty. After he has picked up a dab of molten glass, mavered it, reheated it in the glory hole, mavered it again, picked up some frit—this time shards of flat dichoric glass, which is dark on one side and looks like metallic foil on the other—flashed it and mavered it yet again, he lifts the blowpipe and blows into the end. Because of the liquid state of the glass, Dan needs only to blow gently: "Not at all like blowing up a balloon," he says. I stand at the opposite end of the blowpipe and see the air bubble come into the molten glass and stay suspended there. He is quickly moving away, spinning always spinning the blowpipe, 13 working the glass. Back to the glory hole, flashing more flashing, turning always turning.

Clear glass comes in a surprising form: small, chalky-looking pebbles that are then thrown into the oven. Clear glass is inexpensive, "Twenty-eight cents a pound. It costs me as much to ship it as it does to buy the glass itself. Colored glass is more expensive. Red, especially, because gold is needed to produce the color," Dan says. He doesn't make his own colored glass because of the chemicals involved. Arsenic and cyanide are two he mentions. He purchases rods or canes of colored glass, which are solid tubes of varying circumferences, from Kugler, a company in Germany. "There is a wide variety of colors with varying amounts of transparency or opaqueness available," Dan informs me. "Some glass comes as twisted multicolored canes called *latticino*." 14

Interesting effects are produced by layering different colors of liquid glass and by introducing colored glass by different methods. Adding salt to molten glass produces an iridescent quality on the finished piece's surface. "*Millefiori* is a type of floral-patterned cane class," Dan tells me. "It was first made in Murano, an island not far from Venice, Italy. The methods used for making it were kept secret for over 400 years, by threat of death! Once an apprentice learned how to make *millefiori*, he had to stay on the island." These small canes, a quarter of an inch in diameter, are broken into three-eighth inch pieces and added to the layers of molten glass. 15

As it turns out, Dan is somewhat of a storyteller, and I could have stayed for hours watching him work and listening to him talk. I comment to Dan that it is obvious he is a happy man. "I am blessed," he says. "I get to come here every day and play. Every night I go home and thank the Lord that I get to do what I do. I knew from the very first time I worked with glass that this was what I wanted to do for the rest of my life. I fell in love with it, the romance of it, the beauty of the colors, the immediacy of working with it." As he works, Dan shares stories rich in glass history: the story of Muhammad and his armies building a fire in the desert at night and discovering in the morning light that the heat had melted the sand into glass. Some say this event marks the discovery of glass. Or the story of a glassblower named John Booze who made bottles to store whiskey in. 16

Dan speaks of the loss of many old skills due to the lack of apprenticeships in today's workforce. On that note, Dan shares yet another story about an old glassblower from Niwot, Colorado, whose 17 craft was making prosthetic glass eyes for people. The old craftsman bemoaned to Dan his regret at not being able to pass his skill on to anyone before he died.

"Duck!" my brain shouts, a split second after I hear the first sharp ping, followed by the sound of glass breaking and the sense of it shooting across the studio. I cannot locate the source, and I ask Dan what caused the noise. "As the small amount of glass that is left on the punty or blowpipe begins to cool, it shatters and pops off, sending pieces shooting across the floor of the room," Dan informs me. While it is a startling occurrence, the second time it happens, running for cover seems a bit dramatic; instead, I stay seated and continue to watch Dan work his glass. 18

Dan is a craftsman, an artisan, and a teacher. As we speak of the classes he teaches, he tells me of high school students he is working with: "I was worried about working with high school kids, but it's been wonderful." Dan shows me a clay mask that has a resemblance to his face, mustache and all. "I came to work one morning, and this was on my desk," he says. "A student made it for me." The pride on his face and in his voice is no less brilliant than the shine on the multiple pieces of glass that are in front of us. Dan is touching lives not only by the beauty he creates but also by passing on the skills of his craft to others. He is an inspiration, a mentor. 19

# *Homemade Horror*

**Glenda Sourisseau**

*Mt. San Jacinto College, Menifee Valley*
*Menifee, California*

Imagine walking into a dark maze with walls made of black plastic. Your vision is slightly impaired by the fog hanging in the air; you can smell the straw covering the path beneath your feet. You come to a corner and stop for a moment to consider what might be waiting just out of sight. You take a deep breath and slowly turn the corner. Sitting there is a beastly looking man. His face is pale, and from his eye sockets blood streams down his cheeks. Leather straps tightly bind his wrists and forearms to the arms of the chair in which he is sitting. His ankles are also strapped down. Through the wildly flickering strobe light, you notice the man is shaking all over, and there are sparks flying off of the headpiece he is wearing. The man is being executed right before your very eyes. 1

Startled by what you have just seen, you wonder whether or not you should continue on, yet curiosity prevails, and you once again begin walking, this time more slowly, until you come to an intersection of two halls. As you choose a path, you feel a cold hand on your shoulder, and you quickly turn around to find a horribly disfigured maniac staring you in the face. Your attempt to escape his clutches leads you to a small room full of menacing clowns. They smile in devilish fashion, showing teeth that are sharp enough to cut through anything that moves. Their strangely evil eyes glow in the black light that shines down from above them. And they are staring right at you. 2

Your fears have not yet ended, for as you enter the next room, a partially decomposed corpse throws open its coffin's lid. At this point, your nerves are shot, and you have had enough. You don't even care about the candy sitting in the large witch's caldron next to the corpse's final resting spot. You just want to find your way back to freedom, but to get there you have to pass by a seven-foot-tall werewolf, drooling blood and saliva onto a pile of human remains below him. 3

When you finally reach the safety of the exit, your fear begins to transform into excitement, and whereas just a few minutes ago you wanted to run away, now you can't wait to return to the hellish domain from which you have just fled. You have just experienced a trip through Glenn's Gory Garage Haunt. 4

"It is basically an all-year project," Glenn, in a paint-blotched T-shirt and faded sweat pants, says to me as he works on a skeleton that he plans to add to his collection this year. "When I am not working on a new monster, I am tossing around new ideas in my mind. I drive my wife crazy! She thinks I am completely obsessed." He giggles as Kristin, his wife, shakes her head in agreement. 5

"When did this obsession begin for you?" I ask, curious. 6

"It actually started out as a competition between me and the neighbor across the street. We used to tease each other during football season. I liked one team; he liked another. I would go over there and put my team's bumper stickers on his car and laugh at him for a week until he noticed they were there. He would get me back by leaving his team's banners or other sports junk on my garage door or stuck in my front yard. We did this back and forth for the entire season, and after that, it was a different competition, and so on. Then one Halloween, I decided to compete with his haunted display in his front yard. Within a few years, my neighbor gave up the Halloween competition. He told me I was completely nuts. He just couldn't top what I had done anymore." 7

Glenn Kiehl, a thirty-one-year-old service manager for a major water treatment company, is a responsible and hard-working family man. His stocky build and baby face, mixed with his constant, playful smile, make him look very much like a young boy. He laughs at everything, hates confrontation, and thinks everyone should have a permanent smile on his or her face: "Life should be fun; people should be happy. Otherwise, what is the point of living?" 8

He shows me his extensive collection of ghouls and, with excitement in his voice, tells me the history of each and every one of them. "I couldn't afford to buy monsters for my haunted house, so I started building them instead. I have used some of the weirdest stuff to make some of these guys," he chuckles. He takes me over to a life-size Chucky doll, modeled on the character in the movie *Child's Play*, and he tells me he made the mold of the doll by wrapping his four-year-old son from his neck to his ankles in duct tape. He carefully cut the tape to remove it, covered the openings, and filled it with expanding foam. When all of this was finished, he dressed the doll in an 9 outfit identical to the one the character had worn in the original movie, but not before attaching an electrical switch to the body allowing the doll to wave the knife it was holding in its hand.

His collection consists of an eight-foot-tall animated Frankenstein, a homemade Jacob's ladder with electricity leaping through the air, a huge ghoul that jumps out at anyone who passes by the ticket booth he is standing in, and many, many more. Every one of Glenn's monsters is handmade out of items he finds laying around the house or garage or parts that he pays almost nothing for. Most of them have motors or other parts that he designs out of various mechanical pieces. The werewolf functions on an old water pump, and the rotting corpse in the coffin is attached to a bicycle pump that extends forcefully with the help of an air compressor. The handmade electric chair is incredibly realistic, and the man sitting in it convulses nonstop, thanks to the vibrating mechanism inside of him. Also, let's not forget about the never-ending sparks flying off of his skullcap. 10

"My favorite of all my creations is this ghost," Glenn says proudly, pointing toward the garage ceiling. "She is so spooky the way she floats around." He tells me he used a mannequin's head, which he picked up at a beauty supply store, and covered it with cheesecloth. He created hands for her and hung her from a pulley attached to a slow-running motor. He switches her and the black light above her on to show me why she is his current favorite. The cheesecloth hanging off of her flows like a gown, and her arms move just slightly as she floats around in mid-air. She glows under the black light, and the shadows make her eyes look hollow. 11

"Last year, I took a bunch of PVC pipe and wood and built an extension onto my garage in order to fit all of my new stuff in the maze, and I could have used another air compressor since I had so many things moving and popping out at the same time. I just keep building and creating, though. I don't know . . . maybe I am obsessed," he says with a smirk on his face. "I do have to say, though, just by word of mouth, I have people driving for miles just to check it out or to scare the hell out of their kids." 12

As I begin to pack up my stuff to leave, a young boy runs out through the garage door straight toward me. He is wearing a spooky mask and a cape and is brandishing a glow-in-the-dark play knife in his right hand. "This is Timmy, the Chucky model. He is just as obsessed with all this Halloween stuff as his dad," Kristin tells me. She rolls her eyes and sighs: "Like father, like son, I guess. God help 13 me!" It sounds like Glenn has someone to follow in his footsteps and continue the family tradition.

A creative mind and an appreciation for gore keep Glenn Kiehl 14
brainstorming all year long. His true love is to make fun out of fear, and his gift is the ability to create fear by building creeps out of clutter. Old appliance motors, water pumps, car parts, useless mechanical devices, and so many other things that most of us consider junk are all items that Glenn considers valuable for the creation of his homemade horror.

# 5 *Explaining a Concept*

Some writers claim there's only one rule to writing well: make it interesting. Perhaps this is true, but how does a writer make his or her work interesting? Is there some pattern, formula, or principle to follow? Some trick to apply? Initially, a writer's choice of subject matter is, indeed, an appeal to his or her readers' interests, but subject matter alone does not keep readers involved with a piece of writing. How, then, does a writer capture his or her audience's interest? One way to discover the answer is to read others' writing in order to analyze their techniques and understand how they create interest as they present information.

The essays in this chapter address concepts that arouse a reader's curiosity—music therapy, domestic violence, existentialism, and procrastination—but as you read these essays, pay attention not only to the interesting topics but to the strategies these writers use to draw their readers in, focus their subjects, present information, and establish credibility. Notice how each writer organizes his or her essay and defines key terms. Notice, too, how each writer's tone remains objective, never advocating or denouncing, only presenting. And finally, notice how all four writers effectively use and document sources.

In "Music Therapy," Lyn Gutierrez explores an alternative form of healing that may be relatively unknown outside of its profession. To fully engage and inform her readers, she presents her topic from a variety of perspectives: through its historical development, by explaining a music therapist's training, by detailing where and how music therapy is used, and by outlining a music therapy session. Building logically on each piece of information, Gutierrez provides her readers with a comprehensive view of music therapy and its adherents.

Hobi Reader, in "Battered-Woman Syndrome," forces her audience to address the belief held by some that spousal abuse is acceptable behavior. Reader uses facts and logic to convey the emotional and psychological horror of her subject. After detailing the characteristics of battered-woman syndrome, she poses two questions, fixing her audience to the page: Why does battering occur? Why do women remain in abusive relationships? This is a powerful technique, but the answers, the engrossed audience learns, are not pleasant.

Stefan Sapoundjiev's "Existentialism: A Philosophy of Existence, Time, and Freedom of Choice" focuses on the philosophy's three key ideas. Sapoundjiev places existentialism in its historical context and identifies its advocates; he also uses analogies, examples, and authorities to help readers understand the ideas he has undertaken to explain. By keeping his subject tightly focused, Sapoundjiev presents his topic clearly, without generalization or vagueness.

In "The Art of Wasting Time," Anna Pride explores the universally familiar topic of procrastination, effectively establishing common ground between herself and her readers; after all, everyone has wasted time one way or another. Pride then systematically explores the concept of procrastination and the range of physiological, psychological, and sociological explanations that try to account for it. In addition, Pride effectively capitalizes on the tendency for people to project themselves into what they are reading and to think "That sounds a lot like me!"

# *Music Therapy*

**Lyn Gutierrez**
*Mt. San Jacinto College*
*San Jacinto, California*

Why do department stores play music for their customers? Why does the dentist let patients pick music to listen to while in the chair? Why do companies have music playing for the callers waiting on hold? Why do most people listen to music while driving? The answer is simple: music is therapeutic—it can relax, rejuvenate, calm, and energize. 1

During and after World War I and World War II, musicians visited veterans' hospitals around the country in an effort to lift the spirits of patients suffering from physical and emotional trauma. The performers would sing, dance, play instruments, and perform skits. Doctors noticed positive physical and emotional patient responses to the music; it wasn't long before these facilities were hiring musicians to perform on a regular basis. In 1944, Michigan State University offered the first formal degree in music therapy. The desire to expand the use of music therapy resulted in the formation of the National Association for Music Therapy (NAMT) in 1950. Twenty-one years later, in 1971, the American Association for Music Therapy (AAMT) was established. In 1998, NAMT joined forces with AAMT to form the American Music Therapy Association (AMTA). Today, AMTA boasts 5,000 members. 2

AMTA defines music therapy as "the prescribed use of music by a qualified person to effect positive changes in the psychological, physical, cognitive, or social functioning of individuals with health or educational problems" ("FAQs"). Bruce Martin, a registered and board-certified music therapist working in Vancouver, Washington, defines music therapy as "an arts therapy which has been used to help people withstand pain and provide relaxation and recreation. It is used in every stage of human development, from birth through death. Music therapy is used to maintain, restore, or increase a 3 person's social, physical, or mental well-being" (qtd. in "Sound"). Whether derived from an institutional definition or a personal one, the primary goal of music therapy is clearly to promote well-being.

4 But a music therapist does not simply decide one day to pick up a guitar and visit a hospital. A music therapist must complete an approved college curriculum,[1] including courses in anatomy, psychology, sociology, biology, special education, and music history and theory. Once the student has earned a degree in music therapy and has completed an internship, he or she may become either a registered music therapist (RMT) or a certified music therapist (CMT). The music therapist may then elect to participate in a national board examination to become certified by the Certification Board for Music Therapists. Once board certified, the music therapist may choose to practice in nursing homes, schools, institutions, hospitals, hospices, correctional facilities, drug and alcohol rehabilitation centers, community mental health centers, or agencies assisting developmentally disabled persons, or he or she may decide to go into private practice.

5 Music therapy has been used in various settings in various ways; for example, music therapy has been used in general hospitals to relieve pain in conjunction with anesthesia or pain medication, promote physical rehabilitation, and counteract apprehension or fear. Nursing homes use music therapy with elderly persons "to increase or maintain their level of physical, mental, and social/emotional functioning" ("FAQs"). Schools will also hire music therapists to provide music therapy services that are listed on the Individualized Education Plan for mainstreamed special learners. And in psychiatric facilities, music therapy is used to allow individuals "to explore personal feelings, make positive changes in mood and emotional states, have a sense of control over life through successful experiences, practice problem solving, and resolve conflicts leading to stronger family and peer relationships" ("FAQs").

6 Regardless of the settings in which they work, music therapists follow certain standards of practice, have a number of non-musical goals, and may use a variety of musical tools in an effort to restore a patient's or group's physical, psychological, and/or emotional health. In any field that strives to be ethical and professional, standards of practice help define professionalism. This is no less true of music therapists. Among those practices a music therapist should engage in are (1) individualized assessments for each client; (2) recommendations for or against treatment based on the assessment; (3) written, time-specific goals and objectives for each client; (4) a

written treatment plan specifying music-therapy strategies and techniques that will be used to address the goals and objectives; (5) regular music-therapy sessions, with strategies and techniques chosen on the basis of the assessment and goals; (6) regular reevaluation of the effectiveness of the interventions being used; (7) written documentation; and (8) dismissal of the client from music therapy when the services are no longer necessary or appropriate (Brunk and Coleman).

Beyond embracing the profession's standards of practice, a music 7
therapist will identify specific non-musical goals applicable to the patient with whom the therapist is working. Such non-musical goals may include "improving communication skills, decreasing inappropriate behavior, improving academic and motor skills, increasing attention span, strengthening social and leisure skills, pain management and stress reduction. Music therapy can also help individuals on their journey of self-growth and understanding" (Lindberg).

Music therapists may also use their instruments—their musical 8
tools—in a number of therapeutic ways. For example, they may encourage a person to express feelings and emotions through music. Therapists believe that teaching a person to write music or play an instrument can be an emotional release and improve basic motor skills. Therapists also believe that listening to a song can relieve stress, counteract depression, and increase pain tolerance; singing can improve verbal skills, express emotions, and increase social skills; and banging on a drum can relieve tension and improve hand-eye coordination. Therapists advocate music for counteracting anxiety and fear, relieving tension and pain during the birthing process, and relaxing patients before and after surgery.

Once at work, there is no typical session for a music therapist. 9
The therapist must evaluate each client and the results of each session with the client's needs in mind. Improving a person's musical abilities is not the primary goal of music therapy. There are no specific steps to follow, as every person and each circumstance is different. A therapist must draw on his or her own education in and experience with music therapy to encourage the development of the person. For example, in conducting a group session on relaxation through awareness and communication, two additional music therapists may be involved—one to guide the initial exploration and participate in the primary musical movement, and one to improvise for the second musical movement and the relaxation. The first musical movement, using energetic, rhythmic music, acts as a warm-up in which everyone participates. The therapists encourage everyone, especially new

members to the session, to stand, since once the music starts, individuals may not have the courage to rise and move about. The second musical movement is improvised atonally—to avoid any musical associations—in response to the patients' associations to a specific stimulus. The music therapist will usually allow the individual who is least able to express him- or herself physically or verbally to choose the stimulus (which may vary among tactile stimuli, visual stimuli, symbols, or even quotations) so that the person feels he or she has invested in the session. When each member of the session has shared some association to the stimulus, the playing therapist improvises music—arrhythmically and atonally—to consciously reflect the ideas and feelings expressed by the group or to echo unexpressed, unverbalized feelings within the group. During the remainder of the session, the lead therapist works with patients, ultimately guiding them through a series of relaxation exercises (Priestley 78–81).

In 1966, 22 years after Michigan State University offered the 10
first formal degree in music therapy, Juliette Alvin wrote, "Music therapy has become a more or less recognized ancillary therapy and a remedial means [of addressing patient ailments]. . . . [A] number of physicians, psychologists, educationalists and musicians are taking an interest in the subject" (104). Even today, while music therapists claim that their work improves the overall health of a patient, and "[w]hile there is a broad literature covering the application of music therapy as reported in the medical press, there is an absence of valid clinical research material from which substantive conclusions may be drawn" (Aldridge 83). However, this does not mean we should dismiss music therapy as a valid medical alternative, for while there are few cross-cultural studies supporting the claims of music therapists, within the field of nursing—where much of the research has been developed—music is recognized as an additional and useful therapeutic procedure (Aldridge 84).

Society is constantly looking for new and innovative ways to as- 11
sist people in improving their way of life and bettering their physical and emotional circumstances. Music therapists believe that they offer an effective alternative to conventional medicine.

## NOTE

1. A list of institutions that offer degrees in music therapy may be found at <http://www.musictherapy.org/schools.html>.

## WORKS CITED

Aldridge, David. *Music Therapy Research and the Practice of Medicine.* Bristol: Jessica Kingsley, 1996.

Alvin, Juliette. *Music Therapy.* New York: Humanities, 1966.

Brunk, Betsey, and Kathleen Coleman. "Medical Musical Therapy." Oct. 2002. Prelude Musical Therapy. 3 March 2003 <http://home.att.net/~preludetherapy/medicine.html>.

"FAQs about Music Therapy." 1999. American Music Therapy Association. 4 March 2003 <http://www.musictherapy.org/faqs.html>.

Lindberg, Katherine A. Home page. 20 June 1998. 3 March 2003 <http://members.aol.com/kathysl/questions.html>.

Priestley, Mary. *Music Therapy in Action.* New York: St. Martin's, 1975.

"Sound Therapy Works." Home page. 1997. 2 March 2003 <http://home.pacifier.com/~stwmt/stw.html>.

# *Battered-Woman Syndrome*

**Hobi Reader**

*Southwestern College*
*Chula Vista, California*

Battered-woman syndrome. This is the current name for spousal abuse. Before that it was called wife beating. Before that it was called okay. For eons, a woman was considered the possession of a man. Not only was beating a woman accepted, it was also expected in order to keep her under control, to show her who was the boss, and to allow a man to prove his superiority and manliness. 1

The term *battered-woman syndrome* was coined by Lenore Walker and described in her book *Terrifying Love*. In an earlier book, *The Battered Woman*, she identifies three phases of abuse. The first is a tension-building phase, when minor battering occurs. This is followed by an acute battering period, when intensity or frequency increases. The third phase is a calm period, often with the batterer begging for forgiveness and offering gifts and kindness. This is when he usually promises never to hurt the woman again. Even with professional help, however, the abuse usually continues (Walker, *Battered* 49). 2

Battered-woman syndrome is a very misunderstood concept. Many people are not aware of its widespread existence. Others are not even sure what the term means. Once statistics are reviewed, many are shocked. According to the National Organization for Women, there are more than four million women beaten by their husbands or boyfriends every day in the United States, although most assaults are not reported to law-enforcement agencies. One out of seven women has been repeatedly raped by her partner (United States 3). The statistics for divorced women who no longer live with their abusers show that more than 75 percent of these women are still being battered. The most shocking fact, perhaps, is that there are three times as many animal shelters in this country as there are battered women's shelters. 3

Many behaviorists compare a battered woman's emotional state 4
to the Stockholm syndrome, the state of mind of hostages and prisoners who sometimes undergo a bonding with their captors. The hostages become complacent and withdrawn and are often suspicious of anyone who comes to their rescue (Hickey 9).

The battered woman is, in effect, brainwashed into believing 5
whatever her captor/husband says. She becomes distrustful of outsiders and increasingly relies on the husband's truths as her own. The woman is a creature created by the batterer. She has been told lies for so long about who she is that the lies become part of her beliefs about herself. She comes to believe that she is stupid, worthless, unable to make decisions for herself, a bad mother, etc. She is so used to being controlled and beaten into submission that she becomes the perfect victim. Everything is her fault. Nothing she does is good enough. And, to make matters worse, the abuser is often so inconsistent with his beatings that the woman lives in a constant state of fear, never knowing what might set him off. This fear creates an incredible amount of stress, and the psychological damage that results creates a prison for the battered woman (Walker, *Terrifying* 49). As one battered woman said, "The bruises and slaps would eventually heal and go away, but I'll never forget the awful things he said about the way I look, the way I cook, and how I take care of the kids" (qtd. in Spouza 1).

Many an abuser will not let his wife out of his sight. The woman 6
is confined to the home and not allowed contact with family or friends. The abuser is suspicious of everything—phone calls, mail, looks from other men—even a gesture or look by his wife might mean something is amiss. The man controls all aspects of the woman's life—what she wears, whom she speaks to, where she goes, how much money she gets. The woman comes to feel trapped and powerless as the man asserts his control.

Often the abuser was himself abused as a child. Many never 7
learned how to deal with their anger. Underneath all this aggressive behavior, there is often a scared and insecure man venting the feelings he has about his own lack of self-esteem. The abuser may never have learned how to feel or express anger without associating his anger with violence (United States 5). Or, he may have seen his father beat his mother. A man may also batter because of socialization and the belief that it is a man's role to dominate the family by any possible means. Although these stereotypical "macho" characteristics are more prevalent in certain cultures, wife beating knows no ethnic

boundaries. It is also blind to age, wealth, social standing, religion, and any other diversity of humankind.

Why would a woman enter a relationship such as this? There are many reasons. The first is that the man often doesn't show any violent behavior during the courtship period. He is an expert at manipulation and is often very romantic—the last man she might think could be violent. Another reason is that the woman might think she can change the man if he has already become violent with her. "Once we're married, he'll be nicer," she may tell herself. "When the children start coming, he'll be better." Or: "He's just stressed out now. If I stop talking back so much, he won't have to hit me." The battered woman usually makes excuses from the very beginning of an abusive relationship. Often, she has been in a violent home before and knows the signs but chooses to ignore them. In this way, she becomes trapped in a cycle of abuse, feeling she deserves it. She may actually be comforted that she is getting attention from a man, even if it is negative. And so the cycle of abuse continues. 8

Sexual abuse and degradation are common in violent relationships. Rape is very common, and forced copulation with friends of the abuser also occurs. These acts are more than sexual; they are in fact about control, with the abuser acting from the need to control every aspect of a woman's life. 9

Why do women remain in these abusive relationships? Many times they remain because they are terrified. They have become the victims of abusers. Walker borrowed the term *learned helplessness* to describe the emotional state of a battered woman. The term was originally used by Martin Seligman to describe the condition of dogs that were electrically shocked at repeated but irregular intervals. The dogs eventually became so broken in spirit that they didn't use opportunities given them to escape (Walker, *Battered* 40). 10

The physical injuries suffered by a battered woman are often so severe that they cause bruises, strangle marks, black eyes, broken bones, internal bleeding, miscarriage, brain damage, and death. The emotional injuries are just as severe, if not more so, even if not physically visible. In desperation, a woman may resort to self-defense in order to survive. Sometimes this means that the victim kills her abuser. Unfortunately, many of these women who do retaliate against their abusers end up in jail for first-degree murder because of the lack of understanding of our criminal justice system. The children of these women become orphans, their husbands become victims, and, as always, the woman is guilty. 11

When there are children in the home, there is a 300 percent increase in physical violence by male batterers. These children suffer from a variety of symptoms as well, including psychological and physical harm that is irreparable. Many grow up to become batterers themselves or the victims of batterers (NiCarthy 32). 12

Society has begun to change its views on battered women. Once, the cycle of violence was viewed as the woman's fault, just as it was considered the man's right to beat his wife. Through education and public forums, however, the general public is becoming more informed about battered-woman syndrome. This may be the first important step in stopping the cycle of abuse. 13

## WORKS CITED

Hickey, Cheryl. "Battered Woman Syndrome—License to Kill or Self Defense?" *California Now News* Apr. 1992: 9.

NiCarthy, Ginny. *Getting Free.* Seattle: Seal, 1982.

Spouza, Valerie. *Domestic Violence Info Guide.* San Diego: Junior League of San Diego, San Diego Domestic Violence Council, n.d.

United States. Dept. of Health and Human Services. *Plain Talk.* Washington: GPO, 1993.

Walker, Lenore. *The Battered Woman.* New York: Harper, 1979.

———. *Terrifying Love.* New York: Harper, 1989.

# *Existentialism: A Philosophy of Existence, Time, and Freedom of Choice*

**Stefan Sapoundjiev**

*Western Wyoming Community College*
*Rock Springs, Wyoming*

The twentieth century was marked by two world wars, the Korean War, the Vietnam War, the Cold War, and many ethnic conflicts. It seemed at times that humanity was on a path of self-destruction. Offering a philosophical resolution, a new school of philosophy—existentialism—arose during the latter half of the twentieth century. This philosophy echoed the harsh reality of life in Europe during and after World War II—that human beings are unique individuals isolated in a hostile, indifferent universe. Existentialism's most famous adherents are Søren Kierkegaard, Karl Jaspers, Martin Heidegger, Gabriel Marcel, Simone de Beauvoir, and Jean-Paul Sartre, who coined the term *existentialism* to describe his own philosophies. It would be virtually impossible for a brief paper to succinctly summarize the ideas of these philosophers, but there are a few essential ideas for understanding existentialism: (1) existence before essence, (2) the consciousness of time present, and (3) the inevitable freedom of choice and the responsibility that comes with that choice. 1

The phrase "existence before essence"—the "main premise that all or most existential philosophers seem to agree on" (Dolhenty)—was coined by Jean-Paul Sartre, one of the more prominent figures of existentialism, in his "Existentialism and Humanism." To existentialists, *existence* is the actual "human reality of experience," and *essence* embodies the qualities—reason, justice, and dignity, for example—deemed essential to human beings (Christian 249). To understand this important distinction, one can consider the difference between a robot and a human. The first robots were initially conceived and designed in the minds of scientists and engineers for a special purpose, long before any single robot was produced. In other words, the robot's essence, all the component parts of its structure and operation, came before its existence, its actual manufacture. While this idea 2 is relevant to all created objects, it is not relevant to people because, as Christian remarks, existentialism promotes the idea that people were not projected on a "drawing board" or formed in any mind, divine or otherwise, to attain a special goal, and then created to achieve this goal. Unlike created objects, people create themselves from within (250). Or, stated another way, "You are what *you* make of yourself" (Moore and Bruder 512). And since no two humans create themselves the same way, no two humans are alike. No human has essence until the individual creates who he or she is. That is why existence precedes essence only for people (Christian 250). A robot is ready to take on its repetitive tasks as soon as it is assembled. A person develops human characteristics, for example, trust and love, gradually after birth and goes on to develop more complex characteristics, such as justice and dignity, throughout a lifetime.

Another important existentialist idea is the idea of the consciousness of time present. Being a philosophy of time, existentialism urges us to fully experience life, to live for the moment (Christian 250). We are required to change our routine existence within the present. This change is possible only when we realize that it is up to us to choose how we create consciousness, the self-awareness of who we are as individuals. If we let our consciousness be invaded by moods, recollections, or habits from our past, our consciousness determines the meaning of our present. Also, if our consciousness overwhelms us with concerns and expectations about future events, we deprive our present of its uniqueness and suspense. Thus, our "now" can lose its vitality (Christian 250). But we can still recover the intensity of our personal existence; we only need to realize that, as Christian asserts, "we can make decisions as to how we shall live the only thing that, in the final analysis, each of us actually possess—namely, consciousness of time present" (250). The mid-1970s platitude "Stop and smell the flowers" is a pop-culture resurrection of this aspect of existentialism. Instead of photographing the flowers, identifying the species by Latin and common names, noting in one's journal where and when the flowers were discovered, that is, instead of processing the experience to present to others, existentialism asks the individual to truly experience the flowers: to touch them, to smell them, to wander through them, to make the flowers a part of one's own consciousness. 3

The third idea—that freedom is an attribute of man—is of great importance for understanding existentialism. Free choice and individual responsibility are the distinguishing characteristics of humanity (Stallknecht and Brumbaugh 476). Existentialists do not share the 4 belief of the followers of Spinoza and Kant—that freedom itself is the archachievement of human life. Instead, Jaspers, Heidegger, Sartre, and Marcel argue that people are inevitably free and that, therefore, freedom is not a valuable asset of our life but the state of it. Newton P. Stallknecht and Robert S. Brumbaugh, in *The Spirit of Western Philosophy*, state that people's "inalienable and unavoidable freedom" (477) results in their perceiving that they "cannot choose not to choose" (477). However, and here is an irony, when people recognize freedom as a duty, from which they cannot be discharged, they begin feeling anguish or distress. People may then try to "escape" from freedom and its responsibility by justifying their actions with moral and social criteria established in society (Runkle 124). For example, during the Nuremberg Trials of 1945–1946, a number of Germans being tried for their war crimes attempted to defend themselves by saying they were only following orders when they participated in arresting and killing Jews. But humans are accountable for all their actions and even for their emotions. As Stallknecht and Brumbaugh point out, "for the Existentialist, the man who undertakes to argue himself out of responsibility, who denies his freedom, is deceiving himself and thus, by falsifying his humanity, falling into what Spinoza would describe as human bondage" (482). But the existentialists argue that no matter to what extent we misinterpret our freedom, we continue to be free and responsible for all other human beings.

Existentialism originated in Europe at a time when people felt 5
alone and could not explain or justify their existence. And while a number of different schools of existentialism developed (for example, French, German, Danish, atheistic, and theistic), existentialism never truly developed as a philosophical movement. But authors such as Samuel Beckett, Albert Camus, Eugene Ionesco, and Ingmar Bergman gave voice to existentialism as a literary theme in their works. And while existentialism's themes remain embedded in the world's literatures, existentialism no longer contributes to contemporary philosophy (Dolhenty). It does, however, exist to remind us of a time when the world, despairing, sought answers to its sense of hopelessness.

## WORKS CITED

Christian, James L. *Philosophy: An Introduction to the Art of Wondering.* 4th ed. New York: Holt, 1986.

Dolhenty, Dr. Jonathan. "Subject: Re: Existentialism." E-mail to the author. 15 June 1998.

Moore, Brooke Noel, and Kenneth Bruder. *Philosophy: The Power of Ideas.* 2nd ed. Mountain View, CA: Mayfield, 1993.

Runkle, Gerald. *Theory and Practice: An Introduction to Philosophy.* New York: Holt, 1985.

Stallknecht, Newton P., and Robert S. Brumbaugh. *The Spirit of Western Philosophy.* New York: David, 1962.

# *The Art of Wasting Time*

**Anna Pride**

*Augusta State University*
*Augusta, Georgia*

It is three in the morning, and a haggard man puts the finishing touches on a presentation that he has had a month to complete. A bright young boy scurries around the backyard collecting bugs for his big science project due the next morning. A grown woman packs at two in the morning for her six-thirty business trip. A man disappoints his wife with a gift of socks for Christmas, which was all he could find on Christmas Eve. What is wrong with these people? Have they been stricken with mononucleosis or chronic fatigue syndrome? A death in the family? Why do normal, intelligent people fritter their time away and wait till the last possible moment to do the necessary? In a word, procrastination. 1

This phenomenon defies logic. Every other ugly duty is "gotten over with." We gulp down our proverbial green beans, always saving the best for last. Retirement comes after work, M&Ms after nasty medicine, and a soak in the tub after you scour it. It follows that every other distasteful job would be treated the same way. Aunt Nelda's birthday present, the big research paper, a visit to the dentist, and the cat's bath should be *gotten over with* like our green beans and medicine. For many people, however, they aren't. 2

Procrastination is not just a bad habit; it is a condition of mind that has some serious causes and consequences. Far too often, substandard work is the result of putting things off until the last moment. When we procrastinate, we don't actually enjoy the time we waste. Instead, we add to our stress level by letting a project worry us for an extended period of time. To understand this paradoxical and self-defeating approach to challenging situations, we must assess what the process of procrastination involves. This common practice of wasting time has both physiological and mental causes and effects. 3

The art of procrastinating has been developed by humans as a method of coping. It is said that when faced with an overwhelming 4 situation, we have to either laugh or cry. Many of us, on the other hand, just procrastinate. Daunting tasks tax all our faculties and need to be put aside if we are to complete our other duties. Some problems can be too challenging or too far out of our range of experience. If we started early and devoted ourselves to writing that speech, studying for that exam, or firing that friend, we would have time for little else. The bills wouldn't get paid, the kids wouldn't get fed, and the goldfish would go belly up. When asked to choose between carrying out our necessary everyday roles and performing an overwhelming task, the choice is easy: we do the small stuff.

When consequences are *lose-lose*, we are forced to choose the 5
lesser of two evils. The choice between two situations that each have potentially negative consequences is called an avoidance-avoidance choice by psychologists. According to Rod Plotnik, "as the time to decide in an avoidance-avoidance situation grows near, we often change our minds many times. Usually we wait until the last minute before making the final decision and [then] deal with the disagreeable consequences" (503). An avoidance-avoidance conflict is like having two crying babies to change and only one diaper. After the unpleasant task is completed, we still have one crying baby with a dirty diaper. On these occasions, procrastination is an ironic attempt to save our sanity.

We have all been told that everything has a time and a place. 6
Procrastination is a subconscious way of letting us know that we are attempting a project at the wrong time. All challenges need to ferment in our minds. Procrastination is an attempt to buy more of this necessary reflection time. The conscious intellect understands all too well that the paper is due tomorrow, but all that the brute database will understand is that more time is necessary to collate, organize, and assimilate the three Russian novels that were just read. We often need to mull over the details of a situation before we act. In order to make an intelligent decision when buying a car, for example, we have to consider the range of models, colors, prices, and payment plans.

Procrastination can also be a matter of stalling. The brain needs 7
more time to do its work, so the will begins to filibuster. Just as when we need sleep, we yawn, and when we need water, our throats get dry, when we haven't taken ample time to debate a topic, we feel an overpowering urge to procrastinate.

For every task and for every person there is an optimum level of 8
arousal. This level is controlled by our nervous system in a function called homeostasis, which is "the tendency of the autonomic nervous

system to maintain the body's internal environment in a balanced state of optimum functioning" (Plotnik 63). The nervous system regulates hormone and chemical levels in the body and, when faced with a challenge, attempts to bring us to an appropriate level of functioning. This is why our hearts race when we see blue lights and hear a siren, and why a hero has such steely calm in a life-or-death situation. If this perfect level of functioning is not reached, we often don't feel motivated even to attempt a task. Clearing hurdles at a track meet requires a high level of arousal. Writing a good paper, or drafting a proposal, requires a sharpness not usually present in the routine of everyday life. People who work well under pressure have a high optimum level of arousal. Our autonomic nervous system brings us to the perfect level of mental awareness necessary to accomplish each task. For this reason, we often procrastinate until the appropriate hormonal and chemical levels are reached—that is, until the heat is on.

One can go overboard with this concept, of course. The problems associated with procrastination arise when we wait too long, attempt a project too large, and are too overly aroused or burnt out to function optimally. Such a circumstance is in direct contradiction to the Yerkes-Doddson law, which states that easy tasks require high levels of arousal and difficult tasks require medium to low levels of arousal (Rathus 254). In other words, you can't take a math test when you are stimulated to the point of tears. 9

Many a night I have wondered why I am still wide awake on the eastern side of midnight. I have had plenty of time to complete the project at hand, yet there I sit. Is it because I have single-handedly consumed two pots of coffee? Is it just because I need more time to process the information? Or was the assignment just too overwhelming to complete in daylight hours? Perhaps I can tell my professor that I could not reach my optimum level of arousal, and, thus, my paper will be on her desk by Friday. I can only console myself with the thought that I am not alone. 10

Procrastinators, however, should take heart. Some of the best things in life wouldn't be the same without procrastination. After all, a good wine isn't a fine wine until it has spent some time in a cool cellar. And a quick stew may be "all right," but a stew that has been procrastinating in a pot all day is worth the wait. The French say that you're not a woman till you're forty—is this procrastination in disguise? As long as people don't procrastinate for too long, good things do come to those who wait. 11

## WORKS CITED

Plotnik, Rod. *Introduction to Psychology.* 3rd ed. Belmont, CA: Brooks/Cole, 1993.

Rathus, Spencer A. *Essentials of Psychology.* 2nd ed. New York: Holt, 1989.

# *Arguing a Position* 6

When we write to argue a position on a controversial subject, our purpose isn't principally to express ourselves or to inform others, nor is it to have readers nod their heads in agreement. We want our readers to sincerely consider the validity of our arguments as well as reconsider their own. In order to gain such consideration, there are reliable criteria that we can employ, including stating our position clearly, presenting reasonable evidence, and anticipating our opponents' opinions and objections and responding to them. As writers, we should also maintain an objective, respectful tone throughout the essay. Yet, the biggest challenge writers face when writing argument may be seeing beyond their own perspectives on an issue. Knowing where readers stand in relation to the subject is as important as knowing where you stand. Finding common ground in values and beliefs enables readers to construct a pathway to agreement. As you read the essays in this chapter, notice the way the authors address the criteria typically found in an argumentation essay, the way they appeal to shared values to establish common ground, and the ways they use evidence and logic to support their conclusions.

Thomas Beckfield's argument, "Banning Cell Phone Use While Driving," is sure to elicit both anecdotes and opinions from most readers. Although the cell-phone-use-while-driving controversy is a worldwide debate, Beckfield successfully keeps his argument focused. In a logically organized essay, Beckfield, after his introductory anecdote and thesis paragraph, offers specific evidence meant to demonstrate the dangers of driving while using a cell phone; he then presents his opponents' main argument against the banning of cell phones while driving. And even though his opponents' argument may seem reasonable, Beckfield crisply observes why the argument is fallacious.

Mark Jackson opens "The Liberal Arts: A Practical View" with an emotional appeal and then moves into a logical discussion that draws on both sources and personal experience. At times his emotional tone is dangerously close to alienating readers, but Jackson skillfully integrates his opponents' arguments and actually forges a new position, reflecting a reasoning process that concedes a counterargument and then uses it to temper a compromise.

In "Wolves in Yellowstone," Keely Cutts argues that reintroducing wolves into Yellowstone National Park is in the best interest of not only the park but of the nation. Cutts presents her argument aggressively, yet she is quick to acknowledge the concerns and fears of those opposed to the reintroduction, responding to them with facts and statistics intended to allay those concerns. Notice, also, the breadth of Cutts's documentation. The number and variety of her sources, coupled with her recognition of opponents' points of view, go a long way toward persuading readers that the author may be trusted.

In "Phonics First," Shelly Pettersen argues that phonics instruction develops better readers than does whole-language instruction. Pettersen is conscientious in presenting her argument logically, providing appropriate evidence to support her thesis, considering and refuting her opponents' major position, and maintaining an objective yet courteous tone. Notice also that Pettersen, in her concluding paragraph, expands her argument to suggest that success in phonics is not merely limited to reading skills but will lead children to other, greater successes in life.

# *Banning Cell Phone Use While Driving*

**Thomas Beckfield**

*Mt. San Jacinto College, Menifee Valley*
*Menifee, California*

On February 4, 2002, a driver of a Ford Explorer lost control of his vehicle while commuting on a Washington highway and hurtled over a guardrail into oncoming traffic. The driver of the SUV and four unsuspecting passengers in the minivan with which it collided were killed ("Car Accident"). Until this accident, federal investigators with the National Transportation Safety Board (NTSB) had never "identified use of a cell phone as a possible factor" in a fatal automobile crash ("Car Accident"). 1

Most of us, as either a driver or a passenger, have been behind someone who is driving erratically as he or she tries to use a cell phone. Living in Los Angeles, California, I have seen countless drivers dangerously weave and zigzag in and out of traffic, fight to stay in their lane, and almost lose control of their vehicles as they talk on their cell phones. Such recklessness can be terribly scary, made all the more sobering by the sight of a young child or infant seated in the back of the wayward vehicle. With many lives put at risk each day by drivers who disregard their own safety and the safety of others, cell phone use while driving a vehicle should be banned. 2

Exactly how dangerous is it to use a cell phone while driving? Opinions differ. On the one hand, safety advocates insist that cell phone use in cars should be banned completely. A California Highway Patrol report found that "[s]ome 4,700 accidents in 2001 could be traced to cell phone use while driving. . . . Of those accidents, 31 people died and nearly 2,800 people were hurt" (Bell). Federal investigator Dave Rayburn, the NTSB agent in charge of the February 4, 2002, case, reported, "Some of the issues we are looking at are the fact that the (Explorer) crossed the median and overrode the barrier. The other is cell phone use. Witnesses said the victim was on a phone conversation two or three minutes at the time of the crash" ("Car Accident"). 3

Ever since cell phones became a part of our national culture in the 1990s, scientists and researchers have debated their impact on driving. The most notable research to date was a 1997 study published in the *New England Journal of Medicine*. The study found, in part, that cell phone users were four times more likely to have an accident than those same drivers when they were not using their phones. To clearly convey the findings' seriousness, Redelmeier and Tibshirani, the study's authors, equated the increase to "driving with a blood alcohol level at the legal limit" (456).[1] Redelmeier and Tibshirani also noted that personal characteristics, such as age and driving experience, did not have a significant "protective effect" against the dangers of cell phone use while driving (455). In short, the study provided significant evidence that the driving skills of different groups of people are seriously affected when using a cell phone while behind the wheel of a car. 4

Other studies have also linked cell phone use to poor driving or increased accident rates. Researchers at the University of Rhode Island (URI)—Manbir Sodhi, professor of industrial engineering, and Jerry Cohen, professor of psychology—demonstrated a correlation between cell phone use while driving and reduced field of view. Funded in part by the URI Transportation Center, the researchers chose to concentrate on a specific attribute to measure one's driving skill: the breadth of the visual field to which the driver is paying attention. The subjects in Sodhi and Cohen's experiment wore a head-mounted tracking device that recorded—approximately fifty times per second—where the drivers' eyes were focused (McLeish). 5

Sodhi and Cohen concluded that a considerable decrease in driver alertness occurred when the participants conducted cognitive tasks, such as remembering a list of items, calculating math in one's head, or using a cell phone, while driving (McLeish). The URI researchers discovered another interesting finding: tunnel vision caused by cell phone use continues well after the conversation ends. This dangerous occurrence while driving probably occurs because drivers are still thinking about the conversation they just completed on their cell phone (McLeish). Their minds are simply not focused on their driving environment. 6

While proponents for the cellular industry recognize and acknowledge the relationship between cell phone use and accidents, they believe banning cell phone use while driving to be zealous, that problems associated with driving and cell phone use may be easily 7 corrected with education and training. In 1997, the Cellular Telecommunications Industry Association committed nearly $15 million to educate their customers on using cell phones safely while driving (Koffler). With public service announcements, television commercials, and radio spots, the campaign advocated the use of hands-free devices, such as headphones, earpieces, and voice-activated dialers, as well as common sense when using a cell phone while driving (Koffler). Yet study after study concludes similarly: it is the talking, the cognitive distraction of conversation that leads to accidents, not the dialing.

If we do not change the laws regarding the use of cell phones while driving, countless lives will inevitably be put at risk. In an interview with the *Washington Post*, NTSB spokesman Ted Lopatkiewicz commented, "We expect down the road to investigate more crashes involving cell phones as they come up" (qtd. in "Car Accident"). And while the cellular industry lobby is still advocating the freedom to use a cell phone as an American right, when one's cell phone call made while driving causes another's injury, some restriction on freedom should and must be warranted. 8

## NOTE

1. In a survey conducted by InsightExpress, 23 percent of respondents believed that using a cell phone while driving was as dangerous as driving drunk. While 70 percent believed that using a cell phone while driving was dangerous, 61 percent disagreed with proposed legislation to ban cell phone use while driving, and 54 percent disagreed with the idea that cell phone use while driving should be regulated by the government ("Don't Ban").

## WORKS CITED

Bell, Rick. "Time for Drivers with Cell Phones to Hang Up." *San Diego Business Journal* 18 Nov. 2002: 38.

"Car Accident May Be Blamed on Phone." *CBS News.com*. 2002. Columbia Broadcasting System. 24 Mar. 2003 <http://www.cbsnews.com/stories/2002/02/04/national/main328089.shtml>.

"Don't Ban Dialing Drivers." *Fairfield Country Business Journal* 16 Oct. 2000: 11. *MasterFILE Premier*. EBSCO. Mt. San Jacinto College Lib. 24 Mar. 2003 <http://epnet.com>.

Koffler, Keith. "Outside Influences: Speed Bumps for Cell Phones." *CongressDaily AM* 21 June 2000: 12. *MasterFILE Premier*. EBSCO. Mt. San Jacinto College Lib. 24 Mar. 2003 <http://epnet.com>.

McLeish, Todd. "URI Study on Cell Phone Use Attracts National Attention." *The University Pacer* Sept. 2002. 24 Mar. 2003 <http://advance.uri.edu/pacer/september2002/story2.htm>.

Redelmeier, Donald A., M.D., and Robert J. Tibshirani, Ph.D. "Association between Cellular-Telephone Calls and Motor Vehicle Collisions." *New England Journal of Medicine* 336.7 (1997): 453–58.

# *The Liberal Arts: A Practical View*

**Mark Jackson**

*University of Cincinnati*
*Cincinnati, Ohio*

Many students question the reasoning behind a liberal arts education. But even though they may have been forced to swallow liberal arts propaganda since junior high, students seldom receive a good explanation for why they should strive to be "well-rounded." They are told that they should value the accumulation of knowledge for its own sake, yet this argument does not convince those, like myself, who believe that knowledge must have some practical value or material benefit to be worth seeking. 1

In "What Is an Idea," Wayne Booth and Marshall Gregory argue convincingly that "a liberal education is an education in ideas—not merely memorizing them, but learning to move among them, balancing one against the other, negotiating relationships, accommodating new arguments, and returning for a closer look" (17). These writers propose that a liberal arts education is valuable to students because it helps to develop their analytical-thinking skills and writing skills. This is, perhaps, one of the best arguments for taking a broad range of classes in many different subjects. 2

Other, more radical arguments in favor of the liberal arts are less appealing. Lewis Thomas, a prominent scientist and physician, believes that classical Greek should form the backbone of a college student's education. This suggestion seems extreme. It is more reasonable to concentrate on the English language, since many students do not have a firm grasp of basic reading and writing skills. Freshman English and other English courses serve as a better foundation for higher education than classical Greek could. 3

The opposition to a liberal arts curriculum grows out of the values that college-bound students learn from their parents and peers: they place an immeasurable value on success and disregard anything that is not pertinent to material achievements. Students often have 4 trouble seeing what practical value studying a particular discipline can have for them. Teenagers who are headed for the world of nine-to-five employment tend to ignore certain studies in their haste to succeed.

My parents started discussing the possibility of college with me when I was in the sixth grade. They didn't think that it was important for me to go to college to become a more fulfilled human being. My mom and dad wanted me to go to college so that I might not have to live from paycheck to paycheck like they do. Their reason for wanting me to go to college has become my primary motivation for pursuing a college degree. 5

I remember getting into an argument with my high school counselor because I didn't want to take a third year of Spanish. I was an A student in Spanish II, but I hated every minute of the class. My counselor noticed that I didn't sign up for Spanish III, so he called me into his office to hassle me. I told him that I took two years of a foreign language so that I would be accepted to college, but that I did not want to take a third year. Mr. Gallivan told me that I needed a third year of foreign language to be a "well-rounded" student. My immediate response was "So what?!" I hated foreign languages, and no counselor was going to make me take something that I didn't want or need. I felt Spanish was a waste of time. 6

I frequently asked my high school counselor why I needed to take subjects like foreign languages and art. He never really gave me an answer (except for the lame idea about being "well-rounded"). Instead, Mr. Gallivan always directed my attention to a sign on the wall of his office which read, There's No Reason for It. It's Just Our Policy! I never found that a satisfactory explanation. 7

Norman Cousins, however, does offer a more reasonable explanation for the necessity of a liberal arts education. In his essay "How to Make People Smaller Than They Are," Cousins points out how valuable the humanities are for career-minded people. He says, "The irony of the emphasis being placed on careers is that nothing is more valuable for anyone who has had a professional or vocational education than to be able to deal with abstractions or complexities, or to feel comfortable with subtleties of thought or language, or to think sequentially" (31). Cousins reminds us that technical or vocational knowledge alone will not make one successful in a chosen profession: unique problems and situations may arise daily in the context of one's job, so an employee must be able to think creatively and deal with events that no textbook ever discussed. The workers who get 8 the promotions and advance to high positions are the ones who can "think on their feet" when they are faced with a complex problem.

Cousins also suggests that the liberal arts teach students communication skills that are critical for success. A shy, introverted person who was a straight A student in college would not make a very good public relations consultant, no matter how keen his or her intellectual abilities. Employees who cannot adequately articulate their ideas to a client or an employer will soon find themselves unemployed, even if they have brilliant ideas. Social integration into a particular work environment would be difficult without good communication skills and a wide range of interests and general knowledge. The broader a person's interests, the more compatible he or she will be with other workers. 9

Though it is obvious that liberal arts courses do have considerable practical value, a college education would not be complete without some job training. The liberal arts should be given equal billing in the college curriculum, but by no means should they become the focal point of higher education. If specialization is outlawed in our institutions of higher learning, then college students might lose their competitive edge. Maxim Gorky has written that "any kind of knowledge is useful" (264), and of course most knowledge *is* useful; but it would be insane to structure the college curriculum around an overview of all disciplines instead of allowing a student to master one subject or profession. Universities must seek to maintain an equilibrium between liberal and specialized education. A liberal arts degree without specialization or intended future specialization (such as a master's degree in a specific field) is useless unless one wants to be a professional game show contestant. 10

Students who want to make the most of their college years should pursue a major course of study while choosing electives or a few minor courses of study from the liberal arts. In this way, scholars can become experts in a profession and still have a broad enough background to ensure versatility, both within and outside the field. In a university's quest to produce "well-rounded" students, specialization must not come to be viewed as an evil practice. 11

If educators really want to increase the number of liberal arts courses that each student takes, they must first increase the popularity of such studies. It is futile to try to get students to learn something just for the sake of knowing it. They must be given examples of how a liberal arts education will further their own interests. Instead of telling students that they need to be "well-rounded" and 12 feeding them clichés, counselors and professors should point out the practical value and applications of a broad education in the liberal arts. It is difficult to persuade some college students that becoming a better person is an important goal of higher education. Many students want a college education so that they can make more money and have more power. This is the perceived value of a higher education in their world.

## WORKS CITED

Booth, Wayne, and Marshall Gregory, eds. *The Harper and Row Reader.* 2nd ed. New York: Harper, 1988.

Cousins, Norman. "How to Make People Smaller Than They Are." Booth and Gregory 30–32.

Gorky, Maxim. "On Books." Booth and Gregory 255–66.

Thomas, Lewis. "Debating the Unknowable." Booth and Gregory 797–803.

# *Wolves in Yellowstone*

**Keely Cutts**

*The Catholic University of America*
*Washington, D.C.*

Yellowstone National Park, part of the states of Wyoming, Montana, 1
and Idaho, is the center of a controversial issue. From 1872, when the park was founded, until the 1920s, the gray wolf was an integral part of Yellowstone ecology. But by 1926, the U.S. government had successfully eliminated all the wolves in Yellowstone National Park. But now legislation has been proposed to reintroduce the wolf to Yellowstone. The legislation would allow for a limited reintroduction of several packs of the Canadian gray wolf, which is very much like the wolf that was part of Yellowstone's original environment. The total number of wolves is not to exceed one hundred. On both sides of the issue—those for the return of the wolf into the park and those against it—emotions run high. But once the hyperbole surrounding the reintroduction of the wolves is swept away and one scrutinizes the advantages and disadvantages of the reintroduction, there is little reason to continue questioning the benefits of returning gray wolves to Yellowstone National Park.

One of the most compelling reasons for the return of the wolf to 2
Yellowstone is that human intervention led to the wolf's disappearance. Since humans created the ecological void, we have a responsibility to return the endangered animal to its original habitat. As a member of the federal government's endangered species list for twenty-four years, the gray wolf is the only endangered or threatened animal indigenous to the park not to have its own recovery program (Gallagher 39). Wolves were an integral part of the wilderness of the area now known as Yellowstone National Park for nearly two million years before the United States government sanctioned the program to eradicate the wolf population in the lower forty-eight states (Begley and Williams). Since 1926, when the last pair of indigenous gray wolves were killed in the Yellowstone area, the animal has not been seen in its ancestral home (Plummer and Shaw 105). Without the

human intervention that resulted from hundreds of years of misconceptions and biases, it is unlikely that wolves would have disappeared from the Yellowstone area.

Another reason that it is important to return the gray wolf to Yellowstone is the ecological imbalance caused by the wolf's disappearance. While many of the people near Yellowstone fear that the introduction of a new set of Canadian gray wolves will create an imbalance in the park's ecosystem, the truth is that their presence will actually improve the park environment (Gallagher 37). According to biologists, the wolf's absence has "caused a serious ecological imbalance" (Gallagher 37). Without the wolves to prey on the many elk, bison, and deer, the populations of those groups have expanded to such numbers that they are overgrazing and many die every winter from lack of food (Begley and Williams). The wolves will help keep the numbers of larger animals, such as deer, elk, moose, and bighorn sheep, in balance and remove the old and ill animals from the herds, creating a healthier gene pool. Also, with the natural reduction of grazing animals, the local flora, which has been reduced due to overgrazing, will have a chance to reestablish itself. 3

Opponents to the reintroduction argue that the wolves will kill large numbers of the animals in the park, which will have far-ranging effects. Many fear the drop in game will result in less profit from hunting licenses, meaning less revenue for the surrounding states ("NRA"). It is more likely that with the projected one hundred animals reintroduced into the park, the elk population in particular would drop from 3,329 to 3,165, a difference of only 164 animals (Williamson 58). The wolf predation should only involve the older and weaker of the herds, benefiting the herd population as a whole. The fear that the elk, bison, and deer population would disappear with the return of the wolves to the park seems to be unfounded. Wolf advocate and founder of the Wolf Fund, Renee Askins, notes "the only time that [she] can recall when one animal did in another with such a vengeance was the great turn-of-the-century wolf hunts" (qtd. in Dawidoff 44). 4

In addition to the issues of responsibility and ecology, the challenge of wildlife management is involved in the return of the wolves to Yellowstone. Because Yellowstone is a natural habitat for wolves, and since other areas in the United States where the gray wolf can be found are few, the return of the gray wolf to the park is essential. A total of only 1,250 gray wolves can be found in the states of Minnesota, Wisconsin, and Michigan. The introduction of Canadian gray wolves to the park could significantly change the status of the 5 endangered animal (Begley and Williams). In the event that some new disease should strike the wolf population in the lower United States, it is entirely possible that the only remaining wolves in the country would be found in Alaska (Begley and Williams). Opponents to the reintroduction argue that in Alaska there is a gray wolf population of nearly 5,000 and there is therefore no need to expand gray-wolf territory. Those wolves, however, are for the most part cut off from the lower forty-eight states, and even that territory is dwindling, as people continue to develop more and more of Alaska (Begley and Williams). Yellowstone, with 2.2 million acres, or 3,472 square miles (larger than the states of Delaware and Rhode Island combined), would provide the indigenous park animal sufficient area to increase and thrive, without infringing upon animals outside the park.

The most explosive and emotional aspect of reintroducing wolves to Yellowstone involves the wolves' impact on the lifestyle and livelihood of the people living near the park. Hunters and officials of surrounding state governments have their concerns, and ranchers who make a living herding cattle have fears for their livestock. Each of these issues causes concern for all involved, but even with these concerns, I believe the return of the gray wolf is still the best option. 6

Hunters believe reintroducing the wolves will reduce the populations of the elk, deer, and bison to such low levels that they will not be able to be hunted. The hunters further believe that because of the gray wolf's status on the endangered species list, hunters will be unable to hunt the predator, as they would hunt a non-endangered predator under similar circumstances (Williamson 58). Their concerns seem groundless, for as I mentioned earlier, there is a minimal projected drop in herd populations, and in other wolf-populated areas, wolves contribute to only 6 percent of big-game deaths. In addition, once the wolf population has been firmly established, some licenses might be granted for wolf hunting (Gallagher 41). 7

People are also concerned with how the reintroduction of wolves will affect those states adjacent to the park, since some states depend on revenues from hunting licenses. With the reintroduction, the U.S. Fish and Wildlife Service would require the states around the park to survey the populations of elk, deer, and bison for two years without providing funding, and many feel the extra cost would detract from other wildlife programs already run by the states ("NRA"). While these concerns are valid, the small projected decrease in game populations would be unlikely to significantly 8 decrease the demand for hunting licenses, and the non-subsidized survey would only be required for two years. Most states already conduct these surveys and would only need to conduct them sooner than they might otherwise.

Objections from ranchers near Yellowstone pose a more serious obstacle to reintroducing gray wolves to the park. Many ranchers believe the wolves pose a threat of tremendous financial losses. Jim Magagna said about the situation, "We can lose animals to bears, eagles, coyotes—and now they want to add one more factor. There are few old-timers left who can tell you harrowing tales of wolves" (qtd. in Satchell). Most ranchers hate the wolf passionately, expressing their feelings in comments like, "Why not invite the Mafia to move in next door?" (Plummer and Shaw 104). This hatred stems mostly from folklore about the damage caused by the original gray wolves of Yellowstone before their eradication more than seventy years ago. 9

The truth is that none of the 392 land allotments for grazing surrounding Yellowstone is directly linked to the park. Wolves rarely attack and kill livestock, except in the absence of their normal prey ("Local Heroes"). The numbers of cattle lost to wolf predation in areas such as Minnesota and Montana are one in every 8,000 and one in every 25,000 respectively. In the case that ranchers do have problems with wolves, a wildlife support group, Defenders of Wildlife, is developing a fund to help cover the costs of farmers and ranchers who lose money due to wolf attacks (Skow 13). 10

Finally, the fear of those surrounding the park that wolves will attack people should not keep wolves out of Yellowstone. In modern history, there has never been an unprovoked attack on a person by a non-rabid wolf: in the ninety-seven-year history of the wolf in the Algonquin National Forest in Canada, "[o]nly one person has been injured by a wolf—a little girl who shone a flashlight in a wolf's eye and was scratched" (Plummer and Shaw 105–106). 11

The controversial reintroduction of the gray wolf into Yellowstone is more than just the return of a native animal to its original habitat; it will also involve overcoming misconceptions and releasing the wolf from its mythology (Askins 17). But while people's fears color their perceptions toward the reintroduction, the return of the wolf to the park will help create the environment that existed in 1872, when 2.2 million acres of land was declared Yellowstone National Park. 12

## WORKS CITED

Askins, Renee. "Releasing Wolves from Symbolism: Congressional Testimony." *Harper's Magazine* Apr. 1995: 15–17.

Begley, Sharon, and Elisa Williams. "Crying Wolf in Yellowstone." *Newsweek* 16 Dec. 1985: 74.

Dawidoff, Nicholas. "One for the Wolves." *Audubon* July 1992: 38–45.

Gallagher, Winifred. "Return of the Wild." *Mother Earth News* Sept. 1990: 34–41.

"Local Heroes." *Good Housekeeping* July 1993: 51.

"NRA Questions the Costs of Wolf Reintroduction." *American Hunter* Nov. 1994: 14.

Plummer, William, and Bill Shaw. "Yellowstone's Neighbors Are Howling Mad over a Plan to Return Wolves to the Park." *People Weekly* 24 Sept. 1990: 104–106.

Satchell, Michael. "The New Call of the Wild." *U.S. News and World Report* 29 Oct. 1990: 29.

Skow, John. "The Brawl of the Wild." *Time* 6 Nov. 1989: 13–16.

Williamson, Lonnie. "The Big Bad Wolf?" *Outdoor Life* Nov. 1992: 57–58.

# *Phonics First*

**Shelly Pettersen**

*Mt. San Jacinto College*
*San Jacinto, California*

Would we ask someone to play a piece of piano music before we explained which keys went with what notes or the meaning of the notes? Would we ask someone to drive a car before we reviewed the rules of the road and explained what the accelerator, brake pedal, gear shift, turn signals, and steering wheel were used for? No, we would not do either of these things. We would explain the basics, making sure the person understood what he was expected to do, and then we would ask him to put together the pieces he had learned into a song on the piano or a trip to the store. The process of teaching a child to read is no different. The basic principle is to teach individual parts before expecting the student to perform the whole. 1

To teach children to read effectively, we should teach phonics information, not the competing whole-language method. Phonics information helps children learn to read by teaching them the rules governing pronunciation and how the twenty-six letters of the alphabet and various letter combinations are used to symbolize speech. Teaching children phonics information equips them with the ability to read words and sentences. Once they understand and memorize the letter and letter-combination sounds as well as the governing rules, they can sound out any unfamiliar word, reducing the frustration sometimes associated with learning to read. 2

The study of phonics addresses five major sound-letter relationships: vowels, consonants, endings, syllabication, and miscellaneous relationships. Each area is governed by rules that aid would-be readers in pronouncing new words. Following are several illustrative examples of phonic generalizations: (1) Words having double *e* usually have the long *e* sound, for example, *seem*; (2) When *y* is the final letter in a word, it usually has a vowel sound, for example, *dry*; (3) When *c* and *h* are next to each other, they make only one sound, 3 for example, *peach*; (4) *Ch* is usually pronounced as it is in *kitchen*, *catch*, and *chair*; (5) When *c* is followed by *e* or *i*, the sound of *s* is likely to be heard, for example, *cent*; (6) When the letter *c* is followed by *o* or *a*, the sound of *k* is likely to be heard, for example, *camp*; When *ght* is seen in a word, *gh* is silent, for example, *fight*; (7) When two of the same consonants are side by side, only one is heard, for example, *carry*; (8) When a word ends in *ck*, it has the same last sound as in *look*, for example, *brick*; (9) In most two-syllable words that end in a consonant followed by *y*, the first syllable is accented and the last is unaccented, for example, *baby*. While there are close to two hundred phonics rules, a study by Theodore Clymer argues that the use of 18 phonic generalizations, valid 75 percent of the time,[1] could be the foundation for a relevant phonics program.

But phonics-based reading is not widely taught. A 1992 National Assessment of Education Progress survey revealed that 42 percent of fourth-grade teachers were heavily emphasizing whole language, compared with only 11 percent who were emphasizing phonics. Whole language has been officially adopted as the teaching method in about a dozen states (Clark 456).[2] 4

The whole-language approach to reading encourages students to learn to read the way they learn to speak: beginning with whole words, sentences, and stories. Dr. Ken Goodman, a professor of education at the University of Arizona and one of the whole-language movement's leading proponents, argues that learning written language can be as natural as learning spoken language and that children can learn to read by figuring out the meaning of words in context. Goodman says, "Good readers don't read word by word. They construct meaning from the entire text. Accuracy is not the essential goal of reading" (qtd. in Levine 40). 5

Furthermore, whole language, intended to be learner-centered instead of teacher-centered, discourages the use of any reading books that use controlled vocabularies, as one might find in a classroom that teaches phonics. According to Eric J. Gee, a Utah State University doctoral student who has written on the effectiveness of whole-language reading, a teacher using phonics information would teach the effects of a silent *e* on the end of a word, choosing illustrative words from a basic reader, one whose text uses a vocabulary written with the use of phonics rules in mind. Such a method, according to whole-language proponents, focuses attention on the teacher since the teacher knows the phonetic rules; students must await the information. On the other hand, a teacher using the whole-language 6 approach would not point out the effect of the silent *e* at the end of a word but instead expose the students to several words with and without the silent *e* and allow readers to arrive at their own conclusions about the rule (Clark 444).

In addition, whole-language advocate Jean Fennancy, a member of the National Council of Teachers of English and a professor of language arts at Fresno Pacific College, states that reading is easier when words are experienced in context. When readers using the whole-language method encounter an unknown word, they use the context of the sentence to determine the meaning of the word. If they decide that the word is *elevator* when it is actually *escalator*, whole-language teachers believe readers will still be able to understand the sentence. Whole-language teachers are more likely to ignore errors or miscues because they don't want to discourage the child or hurt his feelings (Clark 444). But one must consider the meaning altered when the child reads "Bob spotted Steve riding the elevator" when the sentence truly reads "Bob spotted Steve riding the escalator." 7

Proponents of whole-language teaching also argue that teaching children phonics, which helps them acquire spelling skills, is unnecessary because computers equipped with spell-check will correct students' spelling errors. This may be so, but good readers use spelling patterns to help them sound out new words. Spelling supports word recognition and builds reading vocabulary (Nikiforuk 42). According to Dr. Carl Kline, a Vancouver-based child psychiatrist who has reviewed numerous academic studies focusing on learning to read, "If you know phonics, there is no way you can be a lousy speller" (Young and Quinn 43). 8

The supporters of whole-language learning believe they have the best interests of children in mind. But whole-language supporters need to step back and take a look at the facts and data that support phonics information as a means of teaching children to read. And while many whole-language advocates claim that they do teach phonics as part of their whole-language method, Rudolf Flesch, the author of *Why Johnny Still Can't Read*, says that this claim is not supported by classroom practice. According to Flesch, the whole-language method does not teach phonics information as a primary method and uses only 20 to 25 percent of the phonic inventory. Children must learn all 181 rules in the phonic inventory to truly receive the benefit of phonics (75). In San Diego, California, scores on standardized tests fell drastically eighteen months after the California public schools adopted a whole-language curriculum. The percentage 9 of first graders matching or beating the national median on the tests in heavily minority schools fell from 51 percent in 1990 to 25.7 percent in 1991. The federal government, philanthropic foundations, and universities have sponsored major studies on reading, and findings have been generally supportive of the intensive phonics programs. Low-income and slow students seem to benefit especially from explicit phonics information instruction (Levine 42). Researchers at the National Institute of Child Health and Human Development now advocate replacing the whole-language approach to teaching reading with the highly structured and intensive instruction in phonics rules (Clark 443).

10 Using phonics to teach children to read makes sense. It is a system of rules that equips the student to tackle any unfamiliar word by sounding it out. The confidence a student will gain from being able to sound out words instead of relying on the context of the sentence will carry over to all aspects of learning. Author Andrew Nikiforuk states it best: "a solid grounding in sounds and letters ensures that children learn to read so that they can read to learn" (42). When children feel good about their abilities to perform basic tasks, they are much more likely to accept and succeed in the larger challenges of life.

## NOTES

1. In other words, if students applied the appropriate generalization(s) to fifty new words, the generalization(s) should help them correctly pronounce thirty-eight of the fifty words.

2. Since the 1992 NAEP survey, California has passed legislation that requires phonics information to be taught in grades K–3; $196,000,000 has been set aside to train teachers in phonics instruction and purchase textbooks that stress phonics for grades K–8. Other states, including Texas, have followed California's lead in returning to teaching phonics information.

## WORKS CITED

Clark, Charles. "Learning to Read." *CQ Researcher* 5 (1995): 443–60.

Clymer, Theodore. "The Utility of Phonic Generalizations in the Primary Grades." *The Reading Teacher* Nov. 1996: 182–87.

Flesch, Rudolf. *Why Johnny Still Can't Read.* New York: Harper & Row, 1981.

Levine, Art. "The Great Debate Revisited." *Atlantic Monthly* Dec. 1994: 38–44.

Nikiforuk, Andrew. "Education—Reading Wrangle: Phonics vs. Whole Language." *Chatelaine* Oct. 1993: 42.

Young, P., and H. Quinn. "The Reading Debate." *Maclean's* 11 Jan. 1993: 42–43.

# *Proposing a Solution* 7

Of the various types of arguments presented in *Sticks and Stones*, Proposing a Solution may require the most sophisticated organizational structure as well as the keenest insight into one's readers. The proposing-a-solution essay is an argument within an argument. Before writers can proceed to offer solutions to the problems they have identified, they must initially demonstrate that a problem exists. Doing so requires writers to understand their readers' knowledge and perception of the subject. Once writers have established a problem, they can then offer their solution, providing the necessary evidence to support that solution. Yet keeping their readers in the forefront as they compose, the writers must also anticipate counterarguments to their solutions as well as entertain alternative solutions, generally accommodating or rejecting them. The essays in this chapter show what writers can do when they know their subject and audience well.

Jeff Varley's "High School Starting Time" speaks to both current and former high school students. After his introductory anecdote, he establishes the problems associated with sleep-deprived students. His solution is sure to elicit resistance, but Varley anticipates his readers' major concerns and responds reasonably, using experts' evidence and data to support his solution.

In "Electronic Medical Records and Privacy Issues," Heather Parker addresses the relative security of electronic medical records and illustrates the possible range of problems that could arise if a patient's private and sensitive information were accessed by an unauthorized party. Although many of us may not consider the privacy of our medical records an issue, Parker's essay explains why it should be, and her solution, which is an array of small measures that add up to a larger whole, is thoughtful and reasoned and helps to allay patients'—and potential patients'—fears of this new technology.

In "Sea Sick," Jacqueline Newton and Cynthia Reinhard illustrate how a single dominant problem, when left unchecked, can spawn multiple problems. Newton and Reinhard's extensive background lucidly establishes the primary problem, and they develop their solution around it. Their rejection of alternative solutions is thoughtful and reasoned. Even though the problems Newton and Reinhard identify and the solution they suggest may be specific to the Salton Sea, a large lake in the Southern California desert, their paper's organization and thorough content are strategies any person seeking to propose a solution to a problem would seek to emulate.

In "The Road to Acme Looniversity," Kirsten Dockendorff takes a humorous approach to identifying a solution to a dilemma that has existed since Wile E. Coyote and Road Runner were introduced in their first cartoon, "The Fast and the Furry-ous," in 1949. Dockendorff winds up with an essay that points out how to reason through a problem, albeit ironically, to reach a plausible solution. Even though Dockendorff relies heavily on humor, she does not allow the paper's content to sidetrack its structure. Dockendorff never forgets she is composing a proposing-a-solution essay, and her completed essay illustrates the fundamental criteria for this genre.

# *High School Starting Time*

**Jeff Varley**

*Western Wyoming Community College*
*Rock Springs, Wyoming*

Ah, sweet memories of high school: waking up at 6:30 in the morning, stumbling into the bathroom to get ready for the day, dressing while still half asleep, munching a piece of toast while listening to our parents tell us that if we just went to bed earlier we wouldn't be so sleepy in the morning (or worse, listening to our parents call us lazy), catching the bus as the sun began to top the trees, and wandering into our first period classes merely to lay our head down on our desks to doze off for the next fifty-five minutes. 1

We never could seem to catch up on our sleep, especially during the week. And even if we followed our parents' advice and tried going to bed earlier, the earlier bed time did not make much, if any, difference in how awake we were the next morning. In fact, for those of us who tried going to bed earlier, we generally just lay there until 10:30 or 11:00 before finally going to sleep. The next school morning we were still as tired as when we had gone to bed later. 2

But recent studies have provided evidence that the sleep patterns for adolescents are significantly different from those of both young children and adults. Studies by Mary Carskadon, a professor of psychiatry and human behavior at the Brown University School of Medicine and Director of Sleep and Chronobiology Research at E. P. Bradley Hospital in East Providence, Rhode Island, on sleep patterns in people revealed that adolescents, as opposed to younger children or adults, actually function better when they go to bed later and awake later. Professor Carskadon's research demonstrates that most adolescents' biological clocks are naturally set to a different pattern than the clocks of most children and adults. 3

The timing of the need for sleep also shows biological changes as children reach puberty. Melatonin, a hormone produced in the pineal gland, is an indicator for the biological clock that influences 4 wake/sleep cycles. Carefully controlled studies found that "more mature adolescents had a later timing of the termination of melatonin secretion" (Carskadon 351). This indicates that post-pubescent teens have a biological need to sleep later in the morning. The impact of forcing people to try to be alert when every nerve in their body is begging for more sleep can only be negative. This discovery has a major impact on high school students who are required to awaken early in order to arrive at school early, for asking teens to learn a complex subject, such as math, science, or English, before the brain is awake is futile.

Tardiness, poor grades, depression, automobile accidents, after- 5
school-on-the-job accidents, and general lethargy have all been identified as the consequences of insufficient sleep among high school students. Yet school districts persist in retaining high school starting times that begin early in the morning, usually around 7:30 a.m. But such an early starting time does not benefit the students for whom the educational system is supposedly structured. How do we resolve the conflict of early high school starting times versus sleepy students?

One obvious solution would be to start high school classes later 6
in the morning. A later starting time for high schools can be a controversial proposal if all of the affected parties are not consulted and kept informed. Kyla Wahlstrom of the Center for Applied Research and Educational Improvement at the University of Minnesota pointed out that "changing a school's starting time provokes the same kind of emotional reaction from stakeholders as closing a school or changing a school's attendance area" (Wahlstrom, 346). Presumably, if parents and other interested parties knew about Carskadon's research, they would be more willing to consider changing the start time for high school.

Some schools have recognized the benefits of later starting time 7
and have implemented a new schedule. One such school is located in eastern Minnesota. In 1996 the Edina School District pushed back the start time for 1,400 high school students from 7:25 to 8:30 a.m. Edina Public School District Superintendent Kenneth Dragseth reported that the later schedule has led to better grades, fewer behavioral problems, and a better-rested student body (Dragseth). Dragseth's anecdotal evidence that better-rested students perform better is supported by research performed by psychologists at the College of the Holy Cross in Worcester, Massachusetts. Working with Carskadon, the psychologists "surveyed more than 3,120 Providence [Rhode Island] area high school students and found students

who got A's and B's averaged about 35 minutes more sleep on both weeknights and weekends than students who received D's and F's" (Bettelheim 557).

In addition to better grades, other positive effects cited by researchers include better attendance, fewer tardies, far fewer students falling asleep at their desks, more alert students more engaged in the learning process, less depression, fewer problems at home and among friends, enhanced school atmosphere, and fewer illnesses (Lawton; Wahlstrom and Taylor). With so many benefits to starting high school classes later, why haven't more districts done so? 8

One of the most common concerns comes from participants in extra-curricular activities. If practices currently often run until 8 or 9 p.m. with a school day that begins at 7:30 a.m., what will happen if school starts an hour later? This is a legitimate concern that would need to be addressed on a team-by-team or group-by-group basis. Some practice sessions could be held immediately after class in the early afternoon. Some activities could convene after a short dinner break. If these activities began earlier in the evening, they could be finished sooner in the evening. The one factor every coach or sponsor would have to consider is how important any extra-curricular activity is in relation to the primary mission of the school, which, of course, is learning and education, not sports or clubs. 9

Availability of buses is another concern for many school districts when any discussion of changing schedules begins. School officials in Montgomery County, Maryland, estimate it would cost $31 million to buy enough buses to accommodate later start times for high school without inconveniencing elementary and middle school students (Bettelheim 557). Minneapolis, which buses 90 percent of the 50,000 students in the school district, solved the transportation problems caused by starting high school classes later by starting the grade school classes earlier (Lawton). This has the added benefits of bringing younger children to school at a time when many of them are most alert and decreasing the need for before-school child care for these students (Reiss; Lawton). With careful planning and scheduling, the transportation tribulations can be addressed in cost-effective ways. 10

As the world we live in becomes ever more complex, education becomes ever more important. It is important that the time spent on education be spent as effectively as possible. It is time to look at school schedules that provide the best education at times that are most appropriate to the students. James Maas, a psychologist at 11

Cornell University, points out that "people are beginning to realize it doesn't make sense to pay heavy school taxes when the audience you're teaching is asleep" (qtd. in Bettelheim 556).

## WORKS CITED

Bettelheim, Adriel. "Sleep Deprivation." *CQ Researcher* 8 (1998): 555–62.

Carskadon, Mary A. "When Worlds Collide: Adolescent Need for Sleep Versus Societal Demands." *Phi Delta Kappan* 80 (1999): 348–53.

Dragseth, Kenneth A. "A Minneapolis Suburb Reaps Early Benefits from a Late Start." *School Administrator* Mar. 1999. 22 Mar. 2003 <http://www.aasa.org/publications/sa/1999_03/lawton_side_research.htm>.

Lawton, Millicent. "For Whom the Bell Tolls." *School Administrator* Mar. 1999. 22 Mar. 2003 <http://www.aasa.org/publications/sa/1999_03/lawton.htm>.

Reiss, Tammy. "Wake-up Call on Kids' Biological Clocks." *NEA Today* 6.6 (1998): 19.

Wahlstrom, Kyla L. "The Prickly Politics of School Starting Times." *Phi Delta Kappan* 80 (1999): 345–47.

Wahlstrom, Kyla L., and John S. Taylor. "Sleep Research Warns: Don't Start High School without the Kids." *Education Digest* 66 (2000): 15–20. *MasterFILE Premier*. EBSCO. Western Wyoming Community College, Hay Lib. 22 Mar. 2003 <http://www.epnet.com>.

# *Electronic Medical Records and Privacy Issues*

**Heather Parker**

*Mt. San Jacinto College, Menifee Valley*
*Menifee, California*

Many hospitals have discovered the advantages that electronic medical records (EMRs) have to offer. Traditional paper-based medical records are often confusing, incomplete, illegible, lack a distinct chronological sequence, can only be in one place at one time, and are often unavailable for a doctor's review (Fischer and Blonde 43). In fact, the Regenstrief Institute; Harvard Pilgrim Health Plans; the University of North Carolina; the University of California, San Francisco; the MacNeal Health Network; Kaiser Permanente's Northwest Region; and Kaiser Permanente of Ohio have all supplemented their paper-based medical records with EMRs because EMRs are always available, legible, and organized (Khoury 34). One hospital with computerized records conducted a study that determined patients were released one day earlier and had bills averaging almost $900 less than patients at hospitals that used traditional paper records. Additionally, "[c]omputerized records also make statistical research on diseases and treatments easier" (Baase 21). 1

Despite all the benefits of EMRs, their introduction and use have been met with some resistance, particularly from patients concerned about their privacy and leery of the new technology. Dr. Mansel Kevwitch, who practices in Bellingham, Washington, sums up patients' unease and anxiety: "[E]ven having a [paper] chart sitting out at a nursing station with a patient's name on it could create an issue" (qtd. in "Urologists" 21). In fact, studies have shown that when an individual is hospitalized, approximately seventy-five to eighty people see his or her records (Baase 61). A patient's medical record is highly personal and can contain sensitive information on alcoholism and addiction, prescribed medications, sexually transmitted diseases, and psychiatric history (Baase 57). In unauthorized hands, this information could be used to isolate or exclude someone from society, deny 2 someone medical treatment, or even to cancel someone's health or life insurance polices. It could also affect a person's current or future employment opportunities and make obtaining health insurance difficult if not impossible. Additionally, many people, regardless of the sensitivity of their information, just don't want the details of their medical histories and treatments made public.

While there is no absolute protection against a patient's file—whether paper or electronic—being compromised, a well-designed and regulated EMR system adds a layer of security measures, such as ID codes and passwords, limited levels of access, audit trails, and encryption, unmatched by traditional medical file systems. Individually, each of these measures is a powerful tool against potential privacy violations, but taken together, they help to make a patient's personal and sensitive information as secure as possible. 3

The first level of security is the implementation of ID codes and passwords. Any person attempting to enter the EMR system would be required to enter his or her unique ID code and password (Baase 61). When an employee left the hospital, his or her ID code and password would be deactivated, preventing that employee—or anyone else—from using it again to access the system. This would prevent situations like the one that happened at Newton-Wellesley Hospital in Newton, Massachusetts, where an employee—a convicted child-rapist—allegedly used a former employee's password to gain access to phone numbers of young female patients and then used the information to make harassing telephone calls (Hagland 20). 4

Although ID codes and passwords are effective, an individual could steal a hospital employee's ID information and gain access to the EMR system. To prevent any long-term use of stolen access information, users' ID codes and passwords could be changed on a regular basis. This interval would be long enough to allow the staff sufficient time to memorize their unique passwords, but it would also be short enough to limit how long anyone using a stolen ID and password could access the EMR system. 5

The second layer of security is to limit levels of access to the EMR system and to grant only certain people "rights" to perform certain functions inside the system and to view only certain parts of a patient's file (Baase 61). Individuals would have access only to the specific pieces of information in a record that they need in order to conduct their job; changing or deleting files could only be done by authorized personnel with the correct level of access, which would be signified by the ID code and password assigned to them. For 6 example, doctors would have full access to a file, including "rights" to enter changes. When doctors enter their ID codes and passwords, the EMR system would recognize them as doctors, granting them full access to files. Billing clerks would have access only to billing-related information, not the entire contents of a file. When billing clerks enter their ID codes and passwords, the EMR system would recognize them as billing clerks, granting them only limited access to files.

Another method of securing patients' records would be to grant 7
access to the EMR system only to doctors. Doctors, however, are not the only individuals who need access to the files in a hospital, and limiting file access only to doctors would require two complete sets of records, paper and electronic, defeating the purpose of implementing an EMR database and also preserving the risk of unauthorized access to paper records.

The implementation of unique ID codes and passwords would 8
make audit trails, the third layer of security, possible. An audit trail is a history of a patient's file. It records how many times the file has been accessed, whose ID and password were used, and when the access occurred. If a hospital suspected file tampering or other misconduct, it could examine the audit trails for any peculiar occurrences. Having assigned unique ID codes to each employee, the hospital would be able to track who made what access and when. Also, audit trails would discourage individuals from meddling in patients' files because every file access and keystroke would be recorded electronically, making it very easy to catch people who misuse the EMR system.

But what happens when a hospital suspects someone is misus- 9
ing the EMR system? Who will take the time to review the audit trails? Of course, hospitals will have to hire information security officers and managers to police the system, which could be costly, but these new EMR employees would replace employees who had previously found and delivered old paper charts and files (Hagland 20). This, too, would limit how many people had access to patients' information.

Within the hospital, ID codes and passwords, limited levels of ac- 10
cess, and audit trails would minimize the possibility of a patient's file being accessed by someone without authorization. The fourth layer of security, encryption—the scrambling of data into a secret code—would protect the EMR system from unauthorized users outside the hospital. Only people with ID codes and passwords would be able to decode and unscramble—decrypt—the files.

However, some fear that EMRs being transferred electronically between hospitals could be intercepted or that a hacker could break into a hospital's computer system. Even if such a breach of security occurred, however, encryption would still protect the system. If the EMR system were encrypted, individual files would have no meaning to an unauthorized user, for without the key for decryption—an ID code and password—the files would be unintelligible and useless. Decrypting information can be a long and difficult process; for this reason, encryption is an effective defense against electronic intercepts and computer hackers. 11

Once a hospital decides to change from paper records to EMRs, the hospital should ensure that its system is fully protected. Implementing an EMR system with appropriate privacy safeguards could be a costly up-front expense, but studies have shown that hospitals using EMRs save money in the long run, due in part to the reduction in traditional medical records staff and prevented lawsuits stemming from violations of patients' privacy (Khoury 35). Additionally, while not every plan is foolproof, the use of multiple safety precautions, such as ID codes and passwords, limited levels of access, audit trails, and encryption, can help make a patient feel more confident that his or her medical records are secure as possible, even more so than with traditional paper records. 12

## WORKS CITED

Baase, Sara. *A Gift of Fire.* Upper Saddle River: Prentice Hall, 1997.

Fischer, Jerome, and Lawrence Blonde. "Electronic Medical Records on Clinical Practice." *Clinical Diabetes* 17.1 (1999): 43–45. *MasterFILE Premier.* EBSCO. Mt. San Jacinto College Lib. 25 Feb. 2003 <http://www.epnet.com>.

Hagland, Mark. "Confidence and Confidentiality." *Health Management Technology* 18.12 (1997): 20–25. *MasterFILE Premier.* EBSCO. Mt. San Jacinto College Lib. 27 Feb. 2003 <http://www.epnet.com>.

Khoury, Allan. "Finding Value in EMRs." *Health Management Technology* 18.8 (1997): 34–35. *MasterFILE Premier.* EBSCO. Mt. San Jacinto College Lib. 24 Feb. 2003 <http://www.epnet.com>.

"Urologists Weigh Pros and Cons of Electronic Records." *Urology Times* 31.1 (2003): 21–22. *MasterFILE Premier.* EBSCO. Mt. San Jacinto College Lib. 27 Feb. 2003 <http://www.epnet.com>.

# *Sea Sick*

**Jacqueline Newton & Cynthia Reinhard**

*University of California, San Diego*
*La Jolla, California*

As we sluggishly trod over a two-foot deep heap of dry, salty earth, we reluctantly inhaled inescapable, pungent fumes. The odor painfully brought to mind images of waste-stuffed pigs' intestines that had been dipped in a vat of concentrated, rotting fish. Choking on the fumes, we clenched onto our stomachs in disgust and closely examined what lay beneath us. Our feet were drowned by crunchy bits of fish skeletons and rotting pieces of almost-unrecognizable aquatic life. We were encircled by a sea of death—the Salton Sea. 1

Contrary to the desires of various groups, such as the Salton Sea Authority, that wish to convince others that the Sea houses a perfectly healthy ecosystem, we are convinced the Salton Sea is suffering from numerous environmental problems: an extremely high salinity level, a tremendous abundance of algae, rampant botulism in the fish and bird populations, and an immense amount of pollution from waste dumping and agricultural runoff.[1] Effectively addressing these problems begins with acknowledging that the Salton Sea is, in fact, being drastically affected by a vast range of problems. 2

In 1901, the California Development Company dug the Imperial Canal from the Colorado River to reach the Salton Sea. The canal's purpose was to divert water for irrigation from the Colorado River just upstream from the Mexican border. Unfortunately, loads of heavy silt started to inhibit the flow of water, and many of the Imperial Valley's residents became worried over the reduced water supply. To alleviate the reduced water supply, the company decided to build an irrigation canal from the western bank of the Colorado River to allow more water to reach the Imperial Valley. But as a result of massive flooding in 1905, "the Colorado River burst through poorly built irrigation controls. . . . Almost the entire flow of the river filled the Salton Basin for more than a year, inundating communities, farms and 3 the main line of the Southern Pacific Railroad" ("The Salton Sea"). By the time the damaged canal was fixed, the present-day Salton Sea was formed. Instead of evaporating over a period of years, as it was supposed to have done, the Salton Sea still lingers because of the agricultural runoff from irrigation in the Imperial and Coachella Valleys (Salton Sea Authority, "Historical").

A high salinity level is the primary cause for many of the Salton Sea's resulting environmental problems. The flooding that originally formed the Salton Sea left behind runoff rich in salt. When the breached irrigation canal was finally repaired, the newly formed Salton Sea lost its ability to circulate water and replenish itself to compensate for the extreme evaporation caused by the Southern Californian heat (Miyamoto 12; Wakefield 8). And even today the "annual inflow to the [Salton] Sea averages about 1,300,000 acre-feet, carrying approximately 4,000,000 tons of dissolved salt" ("The Salton Sea: A Brief"). Incredibly, the salinity level in the Salton Sea is 25 percent higher than that of the Pacific Ocean. The high level of evaporation increases the salt concentration and also contributes to the overabundance of nutrients relative to the concentration of water (see Figure 1). It should be recognized that the increasing salt content and the plethora of unused nutrients are injurious to the lives of fish, and many of the fish in the Salton Sea have died off. As water has evaporated, the salt level has risen to the point where fish are no longer living in an environment they can tolerate. The fish that are able to survive may soon be unable to procreate and continue their species. 4

Some may argue that the concentration of nutrients in the water counteracts the detrimental salinity level and actually helps the fish to live despite the salt. However, the fact is that there is an *overabundance* of nutrients, which fuels an excessive number of algae blooms, which contributes to the high rates of fish death. Algae feed on the unchecked nutrients and break down bacteria found in the water, a normal metabolic process that leads to anaerobic conditions—a depletion of oxygen—in the Salton Sea, creating a hazardous environment for oxygen-breathing animals, including fish (Rodriguez 10). Fish kill-off in the Salton Sea is only exacerbated by our reluctance to address the problem of high salinity levels and an overabundance of nutrients. 5

To address oxygen depletion in the Salton Sea, the government introduced a species of farm fish native to Africa and South America called tilapia that feeds on algae and was thought to be a "natural" 6

**Figure 1.** Evaporating water leaves behind salt deposits and pollution. February 7, 2003.

control to the growth and heartiness of the algae population in the Sea. However, this solution proved to be additionally harmful because, in the oxygen-less water, bacteria known as *Vibrio alginolyticus,* which the algae do not break down and which carries type C botulism, began to live and thrive and infect the tilapia. Once a fish is infected and becomes a carrier of botulism, it forms lesions, its organs begin to swell, and it literally dies from the inside out (see Figure 2). Birds, which instinctively prey on weaker and wounded fish, eat the botulism-infected tilapia and, in turn, die from the fish-borne disease (see Figure 3).

The tilapia not only failed to control the excessive algae blooms 7
and solve the problem of the oxygen-depleted waters of the Salton Sea, they also have become a threat to sport fishermen. Tilapia are popular commodities in the fishing industry because they can be easily caught. When properly cooked and not left to spoil, the botulism in infected fish will die and not cause any harm to human consumers ("The Salton Sea). Yet eating them can be dangerous if they are

**Figure 2.** A fish skull lies on top of fish bones. February 7, 2003.

**Figure 3.** A dead, headless bird on the Salton Sea's shoreline. February 7, 2003.

**Figure 4.** The Salton Sea's shoreline at dusk. February 7, 2003. Note the fish bones gathered along the water line on the left side of the photo and the salt and polution left on the shore at high tide along the right of the photo.

handled improperly. However, not everyone knows how important it is to handle the fish properly. Failing to inform the public of the infected fish and to instruct them on how to handle the fish is immoral. The tilapia that have been introduced to the Salton Sea in hopes of treating fish kill-off by eating oxygen-depleting algae have only amplified the problem by incubating botulism. This potential threat to human life has made the problem of resuscitating the Salton Sea all the more urgent.

The health of the area is further endangered not only by the high 8
rates of fish and bird death but also by pollution. As organisms die, their corpses contaminate the already polluted water and shore. The entire shoreline is covered with the remnants of fish (mainly tilapia—see Figure 4), contributing to the decaying odor characteristic of the Salton Sea (Rodriguez 10). Also, dangerously high levels of chemicals such as phosphate are present in the waters of the Salton Sea. Phosphate, a compound found in lakes because of waste dumping and contamination from fertilizers, causes algae to bloom in the Salton Sea (Rodriguez 2–3). Advancements in technology and dependency

on urban industries have provoked careless dumping of industrial waste products, such as phosphate (Wakefield iv). Along with the high salinity level, unchecked algae blooms, and botulism-infected, dead, and decaying fish and birds, waste and chemical pollution is another factor that has resulted in the downfall of the ecosystem surrounding the Salton Sea.

The many problems that negatively affect the Salton Sea essentially derive from the water's high salinity level. Until the salt concentration is dealt with, harmful algae blooms and dead fish and birds will continue to proliferate. Any other attempts to solve the problem, such as the government's failed effort to control the algae by introducing tilapia to the environment, will only prove to be futile unless the salt level is reduced. Salt has a profound impact on life and cannot be overlooked. Reducing the salinity level has been recognized as an effective technique that would prevent the harm done to the entire environment (which includes bird and fish species), as detailed in the "Draft Salton Sea Restoration Project Environmental Impact Statement/Environmental Impact Report" prepared by the Salton Sea Authority and the U.S. Department of Interior's Bureau of Reclamation. Individuals must recognize the complexity behind the sufferings of the Salton Sea's ecosystem. At the Salton Sea, death is a continuous and inevitable cycle of events: (1) the massive amount of salt weakens the numerous fish that are already harmed by pollution from the runoff in the water; (2) the weakened fish are susceptible to botulism; (3) birds that eat botulism-infected fish are infected; (4) the carcasses of dead fish and birds further pollute the environment by adding excessive amounts of nutrients to the water; (5) when the algae feed on these nutrients, they create an anaerobic environment that further weakens the fish; and then (6) the cycle begins again. 9

Although various solutions have been proposed, some to inhibit algae growth and others to encourage agricultural dumping to compensate for evaporating water, none are as effective as those solutions that directly address the mounting salinity of the Sea. An effective method for reducing the salinity of the Sea, not just temporarily but conclusively, would be to include the Salton Sea in the flow of the Colorado River. Artificial tributaries or aqueducts could be constructed that would direct Colorado River water into and out of the Salton Sea. As circulation of fresh water from the Colorado increases within the Salton Sea, the overall condition of life in the Sea will recover. The reduced salinity level would have a rippling effect on the 10 algae, fish, and birds. The algae would no longer monopolize the oxygen supply, botulism would be less prevalent, and the fish and birds would be healthier. Such a project could be funded, in part, by selling the now cleaner Salton Sea water to surrounding cities, such as Los Angeles and San Diego. In order to end the continuance of death, many steps must be taken, but the first and largest step would be to reduce the water's salinity.

Those who would argue that building an aqueduct leading into and out of the Salton Sea would be too great an enterprise—since the Colorado River is approximately fifty miles from the Salton Sea—forget that more than one hundred years ago the California Development Company dug the Imperial Canal from the Colorado River to reach the Salton Basin to divert water for irrigation. With the advances in engineering technology over the past one hundred years, constructing artificial tributaries to channel the flow of water into and out of the Salton Sea is a practical, realistic plan. 11

An alternative solution to constructing aqueducts would be to construct pipelines or a canal between the Salton Sea and the Gulf of California. While a canal between the two bodies of water as a way of exchanging ocean water for Salton Sea water is appealing and would reduce the salinity enough to ensure the health of the birds and fish dependent upon the Salton Sea, one must remember that the Salton Sea sits roughly 220 feet below sea level. Massive flooding would occur if the water in the canal were not controlled through a series of locks, similar to those used in the Panama Canal. However, a series of locks would impede the free flow of water necessary to reduce the salinity in the Salton Sea. If pipelines were to be constructed to carry water from the Pacific Ocean in and Salton Sea water out, the pipes, in order to move the 1,100,000 acre-feet of water in each direction each year required to lower the Sea's salinity, would have to be 16 feet in diameter and would have to cross miles of rough terrain to reach the Gulf of California, making such a plan horribly impractical ("The Salton Sea: A Brief"). 12

If an individual were to visit the Salton Sea, he or she would undoubtedly realize that the Sea is not healthy. Upon encountering the noisome smells and the nauseating views of the shoreline, the water, and the diseased and dying aquatic life, it is not difficult to believe that the Salton Sea is suffering severely from a high salt concentration, algae blooms, bird and fish kill-off, and pollution in general. The Sea, a gargantuan body of water presently about 35 miles wide by 15 miles long, provides an environment for the lives of hundreds 13 of organisms. Ever since the Sea was blockaded, those organisms have suffered. Because the Sea—and the enormous variety of life within it—makes up a large proportion of Southern California's ecosystem, the overall wellness of Southern California is in part dependent upon the condition of the Sea.

Reviving the Salton Sea is crucial so that its environment can be made healthy, but seemingly no effective methods have been implemented because the problems with the Sea are not taken seriously. Many individuals and groups, such as the Salton Sea Authority, try to avoid disclosing the Salton Sea's true state. The people in control of the Sea are aware that they will never be forced by authorities to spend money to restore the Sea if the public is not informed of the true situation. There are practical solutions that can be implemented, exemplified in the artificial tributaries proposal. The Salton Sea, accidentally formed by humans, is dying. To save it involves similar human interference; the struggles of the Sea need to be fully acknowledged so that proposed solutions can become a reality in order to save its ecosystem.

## NOTE

1. Approximately 75 percent of the "fresh" water that flows into the Salton Sea is agricultural drain water from the Imperial Valley (California).

## WORKS CITED

California Environmental Protection Agency. Colorado River Basin Regional Water Quality Control Board. "Salton Sea." 2000. 16 Jan. 2003 <http://www.swrcb.ca.gov/rwqcb7/saltonseawatershed.htm>.

Miyamoto, Amy J. "Relationship between Environmental Factors, the *Clostridium botulinum* Type C Toxin Gene and Avian Botulism." MA thesis. U of California, Riverside, 2002.

Rodriguez, Ines R. "The Geochemistry of Phosphate in the Salton Sea and New River." MA thesis. U of California, Riverside, 2002.

"The Salton Sea." *Desert USA.com*. 2003. 16 Jan. 2003 <http://www.desertusa.com/salton/salton.html>.

"The Salton Sea: A Brief Description of Its Current Conditions and Potential Remediation Projects." 3 Oct. 1997. College of Sciences, San Diego State U. 16 Jan. 2003 <http://www.sci.sdsu.edu/salton/Salton%20Sea%20Description.html>.

Salton Sea Authority, and U.S. Dept. of Interior. Bureau of Reclamation. "Draft Salton Sea Restoration Project Environmental Impact Statement/Environmental Impact Report." San Bernardino: Tetra Tech, 2000.

Salton Sea Authority. "Historical Chronology." 2000. 16 Jan. 2003 <http://www.saltonsea.ca.gov/histchron.htm>.

Wakefield, Elisha M. "Internal Loading of Nutrients in Three Southern California Lakes." MA thesis. U of California, Riverside, 2001.

# *The Road to Acme Looniversity*

**Kirsten Dockendorff**

*Bowling Green State University*
*Bowling Green, Ohio*

1 With a "click," the television set goes on. You hear that familiar music and see the Warner Brothers logo indicating it's time for *Looney Toons.* We've all watched them, including the many episodes of Wile E. Coyote and his never-ending quest to catch the Road Runner. Secretly, we've all wanted Wile E. to succeed, although long before the end of every episode we know that his hard work will only be rewarded by his being dropped from a cliff, smashed by a falling rock, *and* run over by a truck. As if that's not bad enough, Wile E.'s defeat is made more miserable by the Road Runner driving over him with his tongue stuck out and a shrill "Beep! Beep!" One thing is clear: Wile E. has a problem, and it is time for him to solve it.

2 One of the easiest ways to get rid of the bird would be for Wile E. to hire an assassin. This way, he could rest easily knowing a professional was at work. Wile E. could use the money usually spent on Acme products to cover the assassin's fee. This would also save additional money because Wile E. would no longer have to buy Acme equipment or pay all of those expensive hospital bills that result when the Acme equipment fails. A professional would be a quick, easy, and cost-effective solution. The major drawback is that Wile E. would miss the satisfaction of doing the job himself. After so many years of working so hard to catch the Road Runner, he might want to be part of the event.

3 A better way for Wile E. to kill the Road Runner and still participate might be to get some help from his friends. Wile E. could call on Elmer Fudd, Yosemite Sam, Sylvester the Cat, and Taz, the Tasmanian Devil. By constructing a plan in which he and his friends combine their natural talents, Wile E. would have the satisfaction of being part of the bird's demise. Taz, with speed equal to the Road Runner's, could chase the bird into a trap designed by Yosemite

Sam: a small mound of birdseed in the Road Runner's path. When the bird stops to eat, a cage would drop. Then Sylvester's natural bird-catching instincts could be of use in disabling the bird to prevent escape, perhaps by breaking its legs. After that, Elmer could use his extraordinary hunting skills to finish him off. The only flaw in this plan might be that his friends don't have much of a record of success: Elmer, Sam, and Taz have never caught Bugs Bunny; Sylvester has never caught Tweety; and you know the results of all Wile E.'s plans. The chances would thus seem infinitesimal at best that even together they might catch the Road Runner.

Wile E.'s major problem in his pursuit of the Road Runner never 4
seems to be the plan itself, but the products he uses to carry out the plan. None of the equipment he buys from Acme ever works correctly. It may work fine in a test run, but when the Road Runner actually falls into the trap, everything goes crazy or fails completely. In one recurring episode, Wile E. buys a rocket and a pair of roller skates. His plan is to strap the rocket to his back and the skates to his feet, and thus overtake his speedy prey. The test run is fine. Then the bird runs by, and Wile E. starts the rocket, which immediately runs out of fuel, blows up, or does not go off. If Wile E. used a company other than Acme, he might avoid the injuries he suffers from faulty Acme equipment. Of course, one obstacle to this plan is the cost of doing business with a new company. Since Wile E. probably receives a sizable discount from Acme because of his preferred-customer status, he perhaps would not get the same treatment from a new company, at least for a while. On his cartoon-character salary, Wile E. may not be able to afford higher prices.

Given the range of possibilities for catching the Road Runner, 5
the best solution to the problem might be for Wile E. to use his superior intellect. Wile E. could undoubtedly convince the Road Runner that a dramatic death scene on the show might win him an Emmy. Since roadrunners are known for their vanity, this Road Runner would seem likely to leap at the prospect of winning fame and fortune for his fine acting skills. With such a prestigious award, the Road Runner could do what every actor dreams of doing: direct. He would win not only fame and fortune, but the respect of his hero, Big Bird.

If and when Wile E. catches the Road Runner, the cartoon, of 6
course, would end. Although this might at first seem tragic, the consequences are really not tragic at all. Wile E. would have more time to pursue his movie career and perhaps even teach at Acme Looniversity.

He would have more time to devote to his family, friends, and fans. And he could finally stop paying a therapist since his psychological issues would be resolved. Wile E. would gain self-confidence and no longer doubt his ability as he did when the birdbrain outsmarted him. He would finally recognize his own genius and realize his lifelong dream of opening a theme restaurant.

After years and years of torment and humiliation, it is time for 7
Wile E. Coyote to catch the Road Runner. Although it is feasible for Wile E. to pay an assassin to kill the bird, to enlist his friends for help, or to stop using Acme products, the best solution is for Wile E. to use the immeasurable power of his brain to trick the imbecilic bird. Regardless of the method Wile E. chooses, one thing is clear: the bird must *die!*

# *Justifying an Evaluation* 8

Although it's easy to make judgments, justifying them is another matter entirely. Rarely do we support our judgments with specific observations and evidence; rarer still do we make explicit the standards by which we judge. In fact, evaluative standards are often so deeply embedded in our individual worldviews that it sometimes seems unnecessary for us to articulate them.

However, when composing an evaluation of a film, painting, television program, magazine, or anything else, writers must plainly identify the subject they are evaluating. Writers must also take an unambiguous position on their topics because evaluation essays are a type of argument, and assertions must be precise. As with any argument, writers must provide necessary and appropriate evidence to support their claims. Such evidence is based upon the criteria or standards writers use to evaluate their subjects. In addition, writers must anticipate and counter potential objections to their judgments.

As you read the four essays in this chapter, consider not only the subjects the writers have chosen to evaluate but also the standards the writers use to make their judgments, the evidence they use to support their claims, and the defenses against counterarguments that they employ.

James Rollins, in "The Little Film That Could . . . and Did," specifically identifies his subject, *The Blair Witch Project*, and he also explicitly states the criteria upon which he will judge the film: its innovative marketing plan and its uniquely crafted point of view. He then presents the evidence, precise and detailed, effectively arguing that *The Blair Witch Project* did, indeed, redefine the horror genre in filmmaking and what it means to be scary.

In "May I Have This Dance?" Robert Nava states that initially he was not moved by the painting *Dance VII*, but his reconsideration of the work—based on explicitly stated criteria—led him to "an exciting surprise." Notice how Nava logically organizes his essay, moving, literally, from the larger picture to the smaller. Notice also how he effectively employs visuals as evidence to support his claims and how this enables his readers to participate in his evaluation of the painting.

In "*The Simpsons*: A Mirror of Society," Ben McCorkle uses memorable and specific details from the animated series to provide a solid, factual base for his evaluation. He argues that *The Simpsons* is an effective satire of contemporary American life whose appeal cuts across demographic groups. McCorkle's overall assessment of the Fox series is that *The Simpsons* succeeds in stirring its viewers' emotions, justifying his belief that the show "should be recognized as 'quality programming.'"

In "*Buzzworm*: The Superior Magazine," Ilene Wolf supports her evaluation of the environmental magazine *Buzzworm* with detailed evidence. Her judgments rely on two kinds of standards: visual appeal, and design and layout. She then describes how *Buzzworm*, in comparison to another, less inviting environmental magazine, masterfully weaves together important elements, such as striking photographs and artful visual and textual arrangements, to create a reader-friendly, visually striking, and informative magazine that far surpasses its competitor.

# *The Little Film That Could . . . and Did*

James Rollins

*South Piedmont Community College*
*Polkton, North Carolina*

In an age when movies are multimillion dollar special-effects-driven extravaganzas, to see a low-budget, independent film rise above the expensively mediocre to make box office history is refreshing. *The Blair Witch Project* is just such a film. Produced for a reported ten thousand dollars, *The Blair Witch Project* successfully redefined the horror genre and what it means to be frightened by executing one of the movie industry's most innovative marketing schemes and crafting a unique point of view for the story line. 1

*The Blair Witch Project* is, reportedly, the result of "compiled" footage shot by three film students, Heather Donahue, Michael Williams, and Joshua Leonard, who were supposedly shooting a documentary on the legend of the Blair Witch in Burketsville, Maryland, but disappeared before the documentary was completed; eight months later, a University of Maryland archaeology class found the three students' film footage buried in the dirt floor of an abandoned cabin in the Burketsville forest. The resulting movie is the assemblage of film found in the cabin. 2

About six months before the film was released, directors Daniel Myrick and Eduardo Sanchez launched a Web site that provided background information on the three film students, their disappearance, and the subsequent investigation (Blair Witch Project). The site featured, among other material, pictures of the students' abandoned car, locations where the students were to have filmed, and the bags that contained their footage, as well as the canisters of the films themselves. The Web site also examined the legend of the Blair Witch, detailing the fifty or so deaths and disappearances attributed to her. Visitors to the site were never told that the site was for marketing and publicizing a movie; all the information was purported to be true, even going so far as to have several QuickTime movies of 3 reporters' accounts of the three students' disappearance and an interview with Heather Donahue's mother, Angie (Blair Witch Project).

About two weeks before the film was released nationally, Artisan Films, *Blair Witch*'s distributor, decided to take this unique marketing scheme one step further by airing the pseudo-documentary *Curse of the Blair Witch* on the Sci-Fi cable network. The documentary presented much of the information on the film's Web site, enhancing the authenticity with interviews with Burketsville residents recalling the legend of the Blair Witch and strange events that had happened in the Burketsville forest. Again, viewers were not told that the events were not true or that the people involved and being interviewed were actors. 4

By the time *The Blair Witch Project* opened nationwide, thousands of enthralled Blair Witch hunters and enthusiasts had overrun Burketsville—a real town—searching for information. Some even had set off for the forest in hopes of capturing images of the Blair Witch themselves with their own cameras. Thousands of people visited the film's Web site, and on opening night almost every showing sold out; *The Blair Witch Project* broke box office records for independent films. The legend of the Blair Witch had reached out and seized America, and practically everybody believed the legend to be true. 5

A clever marketing campaign alone does not create a cultural phenomenon. The product being marketed must have substance, and substance is what directors Myrick and Sanchez provided. Believing that what one cannot see is scarier than what one can, the directors crafted an entirely unique story and point of view. Instead of the traditional horror movie's hockey mask–clad, rusty machete–wielding maniac whose every chop and slice into a scantily clad victim is heavily punctuated with a thunderous jolt of canned violins, *The Blair Witch Project* uses the three film students' own footage—images of them panicking, crying, running, and trying to hide and quiet their pounding hearts—to inject a genuine sense of terror, all without a single shot of the Blair Witch herself. 6

To capture this "realism" on film, Myrick and Sanchez decided to have the actors shoot the entire film themselves using an eight-millimeter camera and a camcorder. The eight-millimeter shots were supposedly what the students were to have used for their objective documentary, while the camcorder footage provided more of a subjective behind-the-scenes look at the filming process itself, often capturing the students' heated exchanges and emotional breakdowns as 7 their situation grows progressively more desperate. In perhaps the most famous scene from the film, Donahue proclaims "I'm so scared" as she—fearing imminent death—tearfully records a goodbye message to her parents (Myrick and Sanchez). The compilation of the eight-millimeter and camcorder footage, which jumps back and forth between an objective and subjective point of view, is the film *The Blair Witch Project.*

To capture and record authentic reactions from the actors, 8
Myrick and Sanchez had as little contact with the actors as possible. The actors were dropped off at the end of the woods, given their camera and camping equipment, pointed in a direction to hike, and summarily abandoned. There was no script; all the lines were improvised. Each day in the woods, the actors would receive notes from the directors instructing them in which direction to travel. They would also find clues or situations the directors had set up beforehand. While sleeping in their tents, the actors would be awakened by falling rocks and cries in the utterly black night. The walls of their tents would be buffeted by unseen hands. All of these occurrences were the handiwork of the directors, and all of the actors' authentic reactions were recorded as if they were working on their characters' documentary assignment for film school.

The primary purpose of a horror film is to frighten its audience. 9
After countless run-ins with Freddie Kruger (*Nightmare on Elm Street*), Jason Voorhees (*Friday the 13th*), and Michael Myers (*Halloween*) and their tired clichés and mind-numbing violence, not much movie making has the power truly to scare anymore. However, *The Blair Witch Project,* with its smart and wholly original marketing and filmmaking, transformed the Hollywood horror movie genre. By exploiting a basic childhood fear—being left alone in the woods at night—Myrick and Sanchez, with an original idea and a meager budget, gave America nightmares enough to last through the summer of 1999.

## WORKS CITED

The Blair Witch Project. 1999. 23 November 2002 <http://www.blairwitch.com/>.

Myrick, Daniel, and Eduardo Sanchez, dirs. *The Blair Witch Project.* 1999. DVD.

———: Artisan, 2001.

# *May I Have This Dance?*

**Robert Nava**

*Riverside Community College*
*Riverside, California*

A visit to the Riverside Community College art gallery can sometimes be dreary and uninspiring. Having seen the faculty art show before, I have found that the pieces on display become repetitive and tiresome, with the same artists displaying new pieces with the same style and technique they've used every year before. However, this year the faculty artists have produced quite a few surprises, one of which is *Dance VII* by Gina Han. At first glance, I disregarded the oil painting, thinking little or no effort had gone into creating it. What could be so special about a canvas covered in random blotches of color? On a second look, I discovered what was so exciting about *Dance VII:* the creation of movement through color, placement, and texture. 1

But to better appreciate *Dance VII*, a brief explanation of color theory is necessary. An important tool for any artist is the color wheel, an arrangement of primary (red, yellow, and blue) and secondary (orange, green, and violet) colors that logically blend into one another in a circle, or wheel. From the combination of the primary and secondary colors, all other colors are created. The primary colors, those colors that cannot be created by mixing other colors, are equidistant from each other on the wheel. Secondary colors are those colors created by mixing two primary colors—for example, combining red and blue to create violet. There are also tertiary colors, which are made by mixing a primary color with its adjacent (on the color wheel) secondary color—for example, red (primary) mixed with orange (secondary) will create red-orange (tertiary). The color wheel in Figure 1 shows primary, secondary, and tertiary colors. 2

With the color wheel, we can also identify different color combinations that, oddly and without any notable explanation, are pleasing to the eye. One of these combinations is called *complementary*, which is a pairing of two opposing or contrasting colors, such as red and 3

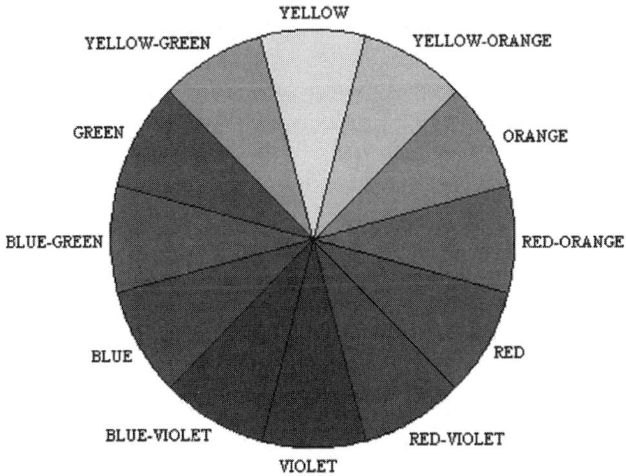


**Figure 1.** The color wheel.

green, blue and orange, or yellow and violet, that are positioned directly across from each other on the color wheel. These complementary relationships also extend to secondary colors so that red-orange, for example, is complementary to blue-green. Another relationship on the color wheel involves *harmonious* colors, which are colors in the same section of the color wheel. The closest relationship, however, exists between a primary color and its secondary color.

Initially, *Dance VII* strikes the viewer as merely a colorful piece, 4
but one of its functions is as a testing ground for color theory, creating radical—but acceptable—color combinations. In Figure 2, the majority of the color blotches are purple, violet, pink-violet, and red-violet, all of which are harmonious colors. The complementary color to violet is yellow, hence the background color. Another use of complementary colors is in the color blotches themselves. Each blotch consists of two "disks" of color, one overlapping the other. On occasion, these colors are complementary: green on top of red, violet on top of yellow, etc. On other occasions, however, the complementary colors are implied or less direct. For example, a little bit of green can be mixed into red to produce a new, toned-down version of red that complements green in an interesting and fresh way.

Another noticeable element in *Dance VII* is that each 5
color blotch is in some way related to one or more color blotches

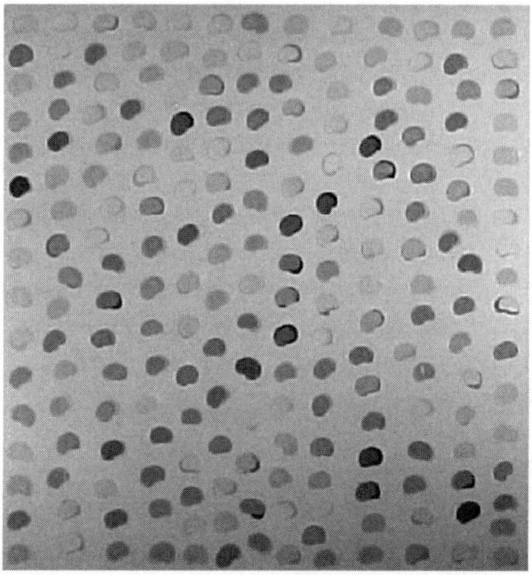

**Figure 2.** *Dance VII* by Gina Han. Oil on canvas (Han).

immediately surrounding it. The two blotches in the center of Figure 3 have a color in common: pink. Han uses exactly the same pink for the top "disk" of the lower blotch as she does for the bottom "disk" of the upper blotch. The upper blotch relates to the one above it because Han has used the same greenish color on each blotch's top "disk." The uppermost blotch in Figure 3 is linked to the blotch on the right because Han has used harmonious violet colors for the uppermost blotch's bottom "disk" and the right-hand blotch's top and bottom "disks." The violet-on-violet right-hand blotch is linked to the lower blotch because the lower blotch's bottom "disk" is also a shade of violet. These playful relationships appear throughout the entire piece, creating paths of color for the viewers' eyes to follow.

In addition to the clever use of color, the placement of the individual blotches is key to the painting's composition. Focusing on the perimeter of *Dance VII*, we see that the blotches are, for the most part, lined up neatly. Toward the center of the painting, the blotches begin to break up and "move around," forcing our eyes to wander around without focusing on any single blotch. Once the orderly relationship of blotches begins to break down, the color relationships come into play, bringing order to a largely chaotic environment. 6

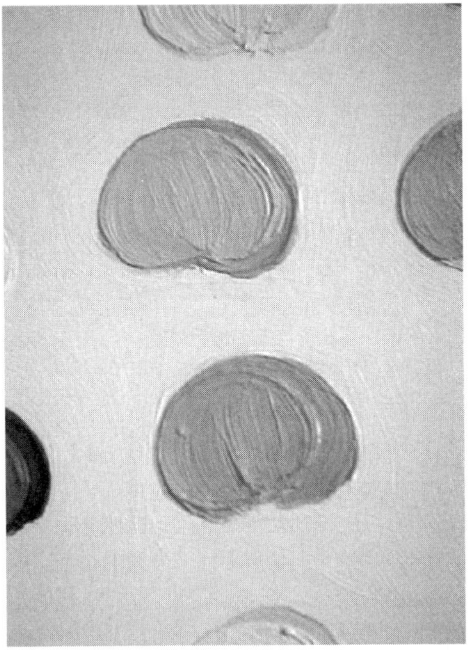

**Figure 3.** A visual relationship can be found between adjacent blotches (Han).

**Figure 4.** Thick applications of paint create texture, adding to the suggestion of movement (Han).

Texture also contributes to movement. The entire piece is smothered in thick applications of paint, and the brushes' bristles carved deep grooves as they were dragged across the canvas. The most noticeable elements of the painting are the blotches, which have the densest application of paint (see Figure 4), but in the negative space, or background, we can see peaks and valleys in the thick layers of paint. These textured strokes intentionally flow around the blotches like ocean currents sweeping against a collection of islands, suggesting movement. The background's fluid-like texture keeps viewers' eyes moving, cunningly redirecting them, again and again. 7

*Dance VII* is an exciting surprise. The painting disguises itself as an unexciting, effortless piece and then jumps out at the viewers if they dare to examine it more closely. The exploration of color relationships initially draws in the viewers, inviting them to participate. But over time, the viewer will begin to see the relationships between the blotches of color. Their eyes begin to move, and they are swept away in a whirling assortment of color and texture. As suggested by the painting's title, *Dance VII* conveys a fluid, harmonious movement among its colors, well-placed blotches, and textures. 8

## WORK CITED

Han, Gina. *Dance VII.* Riverside Community College Art Gallery, Riverside, CA.

# *The Simpsons:* *A Mirror of Society*

**Ben McCorkle**

*Augusta State University*
*Augusta, Georgia*

Over the years, a certain animated sitcom has caught the public's attention, evoking reactions that are both favorable and unfavorable, but hardly ever apathetic. As a brilliant, socially aware satire, Matt Groening's *The Simpsons* has effectively stirred different emotions from different factions of the culturally deadened American populace, and for this alone, it should be recognized as "quality programming." 1

Often, *The Simpsons* is truly brutal parody, hurling barbs of hostile commentary at our materialistic and gluttonous American lifestyle. Many in the audience might be offended by this bullying, except that it seems like harmless fun. For example, when father Homer Simpson decides he would rather sleep in on a Sunday than attend church, Groening is obviously pointing out a corruption of traditional values within the family structure. But recognizing that people don't like to be preached to, the show takes a comic approach, having God come to talk to Homer, telling him to start his own religious sect. The hedonism that Homer extols in the name of the Lord is both ludicrous and hilariously funny, and viewers who might be offended are so disarmed that even the most conservative Republican grandmother is receptive to the comic message. 2

Because it is a cartoon, some might scoff at *The Simpsons* and call it a children's show. But this cartoon is clearly meant for a mass audience, including adults: it is shown during prime time rather than on Saturday mornings, and moreover, it appears on the Fox network, that paragon of broadcast debauchery. The cartoon format allows for visual freedom artistically and, because many people believe cartoons to be childish and incapable of making any real commentary on social values, may aid as well in the subtle presentation of the show's message. 3

The Simpson family has occasionally been described as a "nuclear" family, which obviously has a double meaning: first, the family 4 consists of two parents and three children, and, second, Homer works at a nuclear power plant with very relaxed safety codes. The overused label *dysfunctional*, when applied to the Simpsons, suddenly takes on new meaning. Every episode seems to include a scene in which son Bart is being choked by his father, the baby is being neglected, or Homer sits in a drunken stupor transfixed by the television screen. The comedy in these scenes comes from the exaggeration of commonplace household events (although some talk shows and news programs would have us believe that these exaggerations are not confined to the madcap world of cartoons).

While Bart represents the mischievous demon-spawn and Homer 5
the dimwitted plow ox, the female characters serve as foils to counterbalance these male characters' unredeeming characteristics. Marge, the mother, is rational, considerate, and forgiving, always aware of her husband's shortcomings; younger sister Lisa is intelligent, well behaved, and an outstanding student; and Maggie is an innocent baby. (Could the fact that the "good" members of the family all happen to be female reflect some feminist statement on Groening's part?)

It is said that "to err is human," in which case the Simpsons may 6
appear to be a little more human than the rest of us. They are constantly surrounded by their failures, yet they are seemingly unaware that their lives are often less than ideal. Their ability to accept the hand dealt them and endure without complaint is their most charming quality. Although not very bright as a whole, the Simpsons are survivors. Moreover, they exhibit a patriotic dedication to life, liberty, and the pursuit of happiness that should make every true American proud.

Ultimately, viewers find this family to be unwitting heroes, endur- 7
ing the incompetence and corruption of contemporary education, industry, government, religion, and, ironically, even television. Yet in spite of all the disheartening social problems it portrays, *The Simpsons* nevertheless remains funny. Whenever a scene threatens to turn melodramatic or raise an inescapably deep issue, the moment is saved by some piece of nonsense, often an absurdly gratuitous act of violence.

At a time when it seems that society is being destroyed by its 8
own designs, it is good to be able to hold up a mirror that shows us the extent of our problems. Neither escapist nor preachy, *The Simpsons* provides a satiric mirror, a metaphoric reflection of our dissolving social foundation. More than that, *The Simpsons* is therapeutic: to be able to laugh in the face of such problems is the ultimate catharsis.

# Buzzworm: *The Superior Magazine*

**Ilene Wolf**

*University of California, San Diego*
*La Jolla, California*

Many people today exist within their environment without really knowing anything about it. If this ignorance continues, we will undoubtedly destroy the world in which we live. Only by gaining a better understanding of our planet will we be able to preserve our fragile environment from pollution, hazardous waste, endangerment of species, and ravaging of the land. A new magazine is dedicated to enlightening the general public about these important issues. It is called *Buzzworm*. 1

What makes *Buzzworm* superior to other magazines dealing with the same subject is that it not only fully explores all of the aspects of the environment but does so in an objective manner. *Buzzworm* effectively tackles the controversial question of how best to protect our planet and conveys the information in a way that all audiences can understand. In fact, the term *buzzworm*, borrowed from the Old West, refers to a rattlesnake. The rattlesnake represents an effective form of communication, for when it rattles or buzzes it causes an immediate reaction in those who are near. Thus the purpose of *Buzzworm* is to create a reaction in its readers regarding the conservation and preservation of the environment. 2

One of *Buzzworm*'s most striking features is its visual appeal. Excellent photographs complement the articles. Contrasted with the photography in *Sierra*, another environmental magazine, the superb photographs in *Buzzworm* only seem more striking. The summer 1989 issue of *Buzzworm* features a dramatic, full-page color picture of a gray wolf, which catches the reader's eye and draws attention to the article concerning the endangerment of the gray wolf's habitat. An issue of *Sierra* from the same year also has a picture of a gray wolf, yet it is smaller and the colors are not as clear—resulting in a less effective picture. Whereas both photographs of the animal 3 pertain to their corresponding articles, it is the one in *Buzzworm* that makes the reader stop and discover the plight of the gray wolf.

A photograph must be of excellent quality and be placed correctly in the layout to enhance the article. The reader should be able to look at the picture and receive some information about the article it corresponds to. *Buzzworm*'s pictures of the East African Masai convey specific information about the tribe. Startling photographs depict the Masai in their traditional dress, focusing on the elaborate beadwork done by the women and the exquisite headdresses worn by the warriors. Looking at one picture of a young warrior wearing a lion's mane headdress, the reader gets a sense of the importance of the ritual and of the great respect that is earned by becoming a warrior. Another picture depicts a mother intently watching her daughter as she learns the art of beading. The look on the woman's face displays the care that goes into the beadwork, which has been an important part of their heritage for many generations. Thus, even before reading the article about the Masai, readers have some understanding of the Masai culture and its traditions. 4

Another functional and informative aspect of *Buzzworm*'s layout is the use of subfeatures within an article. A subfeature functions in two ways: first by breaking up the monotony of a solid page of print, and second by giving the curious reader additional information. An article entitled "Double Jeopardy," for example, gives the reader an option of learning more about the subject through two subfeatures. The article itself describes the detrimental effects that excessive whale watching and research are believed to have on the humpback whale. To find further information about what might be contributing to the already low numbers of the humpback whale, one can read the subfeature "Humpback Whale Survival." Furthermore, for the reader who is not familiar with the subject, there is a second subfeature, entitled "Natural History," which gives general information about the humpback whale. No such subfeatures can be found anywhere in *Sierra*. 5

In addition to being an effective way of adding pertinent information to the article, the subfeatures also add to the unity of the magazine. The subfeatures in *Buzzworm* all share a common gray background color, adding to the continuity in layout from one article to the next. This produces a cleaner, more finished, and visually appealing magazine. 6

Once again, *Buzzworm* shows superior layout design in keeping the articles from being overrun by advertisements. I realize that ads 7 do generate necessary revenue for the magazine, but nothing is more annoying than an article constantly interrupted by ads. *Buzzworm*'s few ads are all in the back of the magazine. In fact, not once does an ad interrupt an article. On the other hand, *Sierra* is filled with advertisements that are allowed to interrupt articles, which only frustrates the reader and detracts from the articles.

*Buzzworm* is unique in that it focuses on more than just one aspect of the environment. In contrast, *Sierra* devoted its entire September/October 1989 issue to one subject, the preservation of the public lands in the United States. Although it is a topic worthy of such discussion, readers prefer more variety to choose from. The content of *Buzzworm* ranges from the humpback whale to the culture of the Masai to a profile of three leading conservationists. The great variety of issues covered in *Buzzworm* makes it more likely to keep the reader's attention than *Sierra*. 8

*Buzzworm*'s ability to inform the reader is not limited to the information in its articles. Captions also play a large part. Readers who are too lazy to read an entire article will most often look at the pictures and read the captions. Thus *Buzzworm*'s long and detailed captions are like miniature paragraphs, giving out more details than the terse captions in *Sierra*, which usually consist of only a few words. The difference in the amount of information in the two magazines is obvious from a look at a typical caption in *Buzzworm*—"Finding relaxation of a different kind, Earthwatch participants spend a vacation patrolling beaches and assisting female turtles in finding a secluded nesting area"—compared to one in *Sierra*—"Joshua tree with Clark Mountain in background." Both captions give a description of their corresponding pictures, but only the caption found in *Buzzworm* gives any indication of what the article is about. The captions in *Buzzworm* supplement the articles, whereas the captions in *Sierra* only give brief descriptions of the pictures. 9

Finally, *Buzzworm* is objective, a rare quality in environmental magazines. An article on tourism versus environmental responsibility focuses on both the environmental and economic aspects of tourism, stating that while tourism generates income, it often destroys places of natural beauty that are so often visited. In contrast to this point of view, the article also cites examples where tourism has actually helped to preserve the environment. For every argument presented in *Buzzworm*, the counterargument is also presented. This balance is important, for readers must have all of the facts to be able to make well-informed judgments about controversial issues. 10

Despite all of its wonderful aspects, *Buzzworm* does have its flaws. Some of its graphics pale next to the color photographs. Also, the photographs should be more varied in size to create a more visually appealing layout. Except for these minor flaws, *Buzzworm* achieves its goal of appealing to its readers. In informing the general public about conservation and protection of our environment, *Buzzworm* is far more effective than *Sierra*. 11

# *Speculating about Causes* 9

To see beyond the obvious causes of events is always a challenge. Close examination in an essay that reveals not-so-obvious, even hidden, dimensions of a subject allows the writer and the reader to explore and discover fresh paths to understanding. A common thread in the four essays in this chapter is their concern with such discovery, reflected in the way each is so thoroughly researched and documented. Through his or her research, each writer was able to identify and present plausible causes and offer persuasive evidence supporting the causes for the phenomenon or trend under exploration.

Because college athletics are so prominent in our society, Reese Mason, in "Basketball and the Urban Poor," doesn't need to convince readers that the phenomenon he wishes to investigate exists. By focusing on the death of college basketball star Hank Gathers, Mason uses one specific incident to hook readers into the broader phenomenon he explores: why a person would risk his life for a game. Mason presents a logical sequence of causes—success, education, and money—in developing an essay that ultimately identifies one remote causal connection: the desire to achieve the American dream.

In "What Makes a Serial Killer?" La Donna Beaty proposes a range of causes for this unsettling social problem. Through her research, Beaty is able to make clear the multidimensional nature of this phenomenon and its causes; her essay illustrates that at times there may be no single, simple answer. She shows us that as writers speculating about causes, we must be willing to think broadly about what lies behind an event and not merely embrace the obvious.

The sequencing of causes in Sarah West's "The Rise of Reported Incidents of Workplace Sexual Harassment" enables her readers to progress methodically through her essay. By citing source materials that range from daily newspapers to specialized journals to Internet sites, West intelligibly speculates on four would-be causes. Readers should pay attention to how well West critically analyzes and weighs the plausibility of each possibility.

Krista Gonnerman's search for causes for the pharmaceutical industry's enormous spending increase in direct-to-consumer television advertising after 1997 yields few possibilities, but her supporting evidence allows readers to feel confident that her discoveries are, indeed, quite plausible. Moreover, Gonnerman's evidence supporting her primary and secondary causes is sufficiently compelling that the need to anticipate counterarguments to her own causes is unnecessary. And as a reader of a speculating-about-causes essay would expect, Gonnerman anticipates her audience's suggestion of alternative causes, identifies two, and explains why they cannot be supported.

# *Basketball and the Urban Poor*

**Reese Mason**

*University of California, Riverside*
*Riverside, California*

*For a while there, Gathers had beaten the system, the cycle that traps so many black youths in frustration and poverty.*
—Art Spander

On the evening of March 4, 1990, much like any other night, I sat in my living room fixed to the television as ESPN's *SportsCenter* broadcast the day's sporting news. The lead story was about the 1989 national leader in rebounding and scoring in collegiate basketball, Loyola Marymount's Hank Gathers. It was not unusual for Gathers to be in the news, given his many fantastic performances and displays of great character. He had become much more than a premier basketball player since achieving athletic stardom. Yes, Hank Gathers had become an inspiration to all those who, like himself, had the misfortune of being born poor. This story, however, was not about a new scoring record or a buzzer-beating shot. Nor was it a commentary on how Gathers had not forgotten what community he hailed from, and how he intended to move his mother and son out of poverty when he made it to the "Show" (Almond). This news story was about a twenty-three-year-old basketball player collapsing and dying on the court. 1

In utter dismay, I immediately demanded some reason for the unbelievable events. After an incident some three months earlier, Gathers had been tested and found to have cardiomyopathy (a type of arrhythmia). How in the world could the doctors have allowed him to continue playing? With such a heart defect, how could he allow himself to continue playing? How could the game of basketball have become more important to Hank Gathers than life itself? The night of March 4 was a sleepless one for me. I lay awake in restless wonder at what could have compelled a man of my age to risk his life for a game. 2

The answers came to me the next day in a follow-up story about the tragic death. The piece was a tribute to the life of Hank Gathers. Appropriately, the story began where Gathers's life began, and suddenly, with one shot of the camera, I understood. I understood what drove him to greatness on the basketball court. I understood what compelled Gathers to continue playing even after he knew he had a heart defect. Like most middle-class sports fanatics, I was well aware that many African American athletes come from the inner city. I was even aware that Gathers had risen out of a Philadelphia ghetto to achieve greatness in college basketball. Never, though, had I really sat down and considered why growing up in the ghetto might make the game of basketball seem so important—and, in Gathers's case, as valuable as life itself. 3

Basketball is popular among the urban poor because it is virtually the only way for young African American men to make it, to become idolized superstars. Unlike football or baseball, basketball requires little money or formal organization to play. All that is needed is a few dollars for a ball and access to a hoop, found at any schoolyard or playground. Additionally, it can be practiced and all but perfected without a need for coaches, expensive facilities, or even many other players. 4

The examples of basketball stars like Magic Johnson and Michael Jordan probably inspired Gathers, as they have thousands of others who cling to the game of basketball as their ticket out of the ghetto. There aren't many alternatives. The unemployment rate for African American teenagers is over 40 percent, and what work they can find is mostly low-paying, dead-end jobs. Many inner-city youth resort to drugs and crime, and not surprisingly, about a quarter of all African American men between twenty and twenty-nine wind up in jail, on parole, or on probation (United States). 5

Our society offers those who can play basketball well an education that might not otherwise be obtained. Education is a limited and insufficient resource to the urban poor. There are no easy answers, I admit, but the facts are indisputable. In order to get a quality education, the poor have to win scholarships. Because of its popularity in the United States, and its college connection, basketball has become one avenue to a higher education. Even when college basketball players are unable to continue playing in the pros, their university degrees may lead to other good jobs and thus to economic success. 6

Yet, education is not the motivating factor behind the success stories of the poor any more than it is among the success stories of 7 the middle class; money is. After all, money is what you are judged on here in the United States, along with popular recognition. Basketball provides an avenue from the urban ghetto to the highest echelons in the United States via money and popularity. Gathers was honest about what was important to him when he said, "I'm in college to play basketball. The degree is important to me, but not that important" (Hudson and Almond). Basketball offered him money, education, and popularity—the three components of the American dream. But was the dream worth his life?

We recognize Hank Gathers's tragic death only because he was a fantastic basketball player. It is hard for us to admit, but who would have taken time out for Gathers and his family had he died of a heart defect while playing ball in the Rowand Rosen housing project where his family still lives? Those who were close to him, assuredly, but not the nation. This is why basketball was so important to Gathers, and it may be why he continued playing despite the risk of dying on the court. Hank Gathers's story helps us see why basketball is so popular among, and dominated by, the urban poor. Basketball is an E-Ticket out of the ghetto, one of the best available means of getting nationwide recognition and providing for their families. 8

## WORKS CITED

Almond, Elliot. "Gathers, Pepperdine's Lewis Had Special Bond." *Los Angeles Times* 7 Mar. 1990: C8.

Hudson, Maryann, and Elliot Almond. "Gathers Suit Asks for $32.5 Million." *Los Angeles Times* 21 Apr. 1990: C1, C20.

Spander, Art. "Who's to Blame for Gathers' Tragic Death?" *Sporting News* 19 Mar. 1990: 5.

United States. Census Bureau. *Statistical Abstract of the United States, 1989.* Washington: GPO, 1989.

# *What Makes a Serial Killer?*

**La Donna Beaty**

*Sinclair Community College*
*Dayton, Ohio*

Jeffrey Dahmer, John Wayne Gacy, Mark Allen Smith, Richard Chase, Ted Bundy—the list goes on and on. These five men alone have been responsible for at least ninety deaths, and many suspect that their victims may total twice that number. They are serial killers, the most feared and hated of criminals. What deep, hidden secret makes them lust for blood? What can possibly motivate a person to kill over and over again with no guilt, no remorse, no hint of human compassion? What makes a serial killer? 1

Serial killings are not a new phenomenon. In 1798, for example, Micajah and Wiley Harpe traveled the backwoods of Kentucky and Tennessee in a violent, year-long killing spree that left at least twenty—and possibly as many as thirty-eight—men, women, and children dead. Their crimes were especially chilling as they seemed particularly to enjoy grabbing small children by the ankles and smashing their heads against trees (Holmes and DeBurger 28). In modern society, however, serial killings have grown to near epidemic proportions. Ann Rule, a respected author and expert on serial murders, stated in a seminar at the University of Louisville on serial murder that between 3,500 and 5,000 people become victims of serial murder each year in the United States alone (qtd. in Holmes and DeBurger 21). Many others estimate that there are close to 350 serial killers currently at large in our society (Holmes and DeBurger 22). 2

Fascination with murder and murderers is not new, but researchers in recent years have made great strides in determining the characteristics of criminals. Looking back, we can see how naive early experts were in their evaluations: in 1911, for example, Italian criminologist Cesare Lombrosco concluded that "murderers as a group [are] biologically degenerate [with] bloodshot eyes, aquiline noses, curly black hair, strong jaws, big ears, thin lips, and menacing grins" 3 (qtd. in Lunde 84). Today, however, we don't expect killers to have fangs that drip human blood, and many realize that the boy-next-door may be doing more than woodworking in his basement. While there are no specific physical characteristics shared by all serial killers, they are almost always male, and 92 percent are white. Most are between the ages of twenty-five and thirty-five and often physically attractive. While they may hold a job, many switch employment frequently as they become easily frustrated when advancement does not come as quickly as expected. They tend to believe that they are entitled to whatever they desire but feel that they should have to exert no effort to attain their goals (Samenow 88, 96). What could possibly turn attractive, ambitious human beings into cold-blooded monsters?

One popular theory suggests that many murderers are the product of our violent society. Our culture tends to approve of violence and find it acceptable, even preferable, in many circumstances (Holmes and DeBurger 27). According to research done in 1970, one out of every four men and one out of every six women believed that it was appropriate for a husband to hit his wife under certain conditions (Holmes and DeBurger 33). This emphasis on violence is especially prevalent in television programs. Violence occurs in 80 percent of all prime-time shows, while cartoons, presumably made for children, average eighteen violent acts per hour. It is estimated that by the age of eighteen, the average child will have viewed more than 16,000 television murders (Holmes and DeBurger 34). Some experts feel that children demonstrate increasingly aggressive behavior with each violent act they view and become so accustomed to violence that these acts seem normal (Lunde 15, 35). In fact, most serial killers do begin to show patterns of aggressive behavior at a young age. It is, therefore, possible that after viewing increasing amounts of violence, such children determine that this is acceptable behavior; when they are then punished for similar actions, they may become confused and angry and eventually lash out by committing horrible, violent acts. 4

Another theory concentrates on the family atmosphere into which the serial killer is born. Most killers state that they experienced psychological abuse as children and never established good relationships with the male figures in their lives (Ressler, Burgess, and Douglas 19). As children, they were often rejected by their parents and received little nurturing (Lunde 94; Holmes and DeBurger 64–70). It has also been established that the families of serial killers 5 often move repeatedly, never allowing the child to feel a sense of stability; in many cases, they are also forced to live outside the family home before reaching the age of eighteen (Ressler, Burgess, and Douglas 19–20). Our culture's tolerance for violence may overlap with such family dynamics: with 79 percent of the population believing that slapping a twelve-year-old is either necessary, normal, or good, it is no wonder that serial killers relate tales of physical abuse and view themselves as the "black sheep" of the family (Holmes and DeBurger 30; Ressler, Burgess, and Douglas 19–20). They may even, perhaps unconsciously, assume this same role in society.

While the foregoing analysis portrays the serial killer as a lost, 6
lonely, abused little child, another theory, based on the same information, gives an entirely different view. In this analysis, the killer is indeed rejected by his family but only after being repeatedly defiant, sneaky, and threatening. As the child's lies and destructiveness increase, the parents give him the distance he seems to want in order to maintain a small amount of domestic peace (Samenow 13). This interpretation suggests that the killer shapes his parents much more than his parents shape him. It also denies that the media can influence a child's mind and turn him into something that he doesn't already long to be. Since most children view similar amounts of violence, the argument goes, a responsible child filters what he sees and will not resort to criminal activity no matter how acceptable it seems to be (Samenow 15–18). In 1930, the noted psychologist Alfred Adler seemed to find this true of any criminal. As he put it, "With criminals it is different: they have a private logic, a private intelligence. They are suffering from a wrong outlook upon the world, a wrong estimate of their own importance and the importance of other people" (qtd. in Samenow 20).

Most people agree that Jeffrey Dahmer or Ted Bundy had to be 7
"crazy" to commit horrendous multiple murders, and scientists have long maintained that serial killers are indeed mentally disturbed (Lunde 48). While the percentage of murders committed by mental hospital patients is much lower than that among the general population, it cannot be ignored that the rise in serial killings happened at almost the same time as the deinstitutionalization movement in the mental health care system during the 1960s (Lunde 35; Markman and Bosco 266). While reform was greatly needed in the mental health care system, it has now become nearly impossible to hospitalize those with severe problems. In the United States, people have a constitutional right to remain mentally ill. Involuntary commitment

can only be accomplished if the person is deemed dangerous to himself or others or is gravely disabled. However, "[a]ccording to the way that the law is interpreted, if you can go to the mailbox to pick up your Social Security check, you're not gravely disabled even if you think you're living on Mars"; even if a patient is thought to be dangerous, he cannot be held longer than ninety days unless it can be proved that the patient actually committed dangerous acts while in the hospital (Markman and Bosco 267). Many of the most heinous criminals have had long histories of mental illness but could not be hospitalized due to these stringent requirements. Richard Chase, the notorious Vampire of Sacramento, believed that he needed blood in order to survive, and while in the care of a psychiatric hospital, he often killed birds and other small animals in order to quench this thirst. When he was released, he went on to kill eight people, one of them an eighteen-month-old baby (Biondi and Hecox 206). Edmund Kemper was equally insane. At the age of fifteen he killed both of his grandparents and then spent five years in a psychiatric facility. Doctors determined that he was "cured" and released him into an unsuspecting society. He killed eight women, including his own mother (Lunde 53–56). The world was soon to be disturbed by a cataclysmic earthquake, and Herbert Mullin knew that he had been appointed by God to prevent the catastrophe. The fervor of his religious delusion resulted in a death toll of thirteen (Lunde 63–81). All of these men had been treated for their mental disorders, and all were released by doctors who did not have enough proof to hold them against their will.

Recently, studies have given increasing consideration to the ge- 8
netic makeup of serial killers. The connection between biology and behavior is strengthened by research in which scientists have been able to develop a violently aggressive strain of mice simply through selective inbreeding (Taylor 23). These studies have caused scientists to become increasingly interested in the limbic system of the brain, which houses the amygdala, an almond-shaped structure located in the front of the temporal lobe. It has long been known that surgically altering that portion of the brain, in an operation known as a lobotomy, is one way of controlling behavior. This surgery was used frequently in the 1960s but has since been discontinued as it also erases most of a person's personality. More recent developments, however, have shown that temporal lobe epilepsy causes electrical impulses to be discharged directly into the amygdala. When this electronic stimulation is re-created in the laboratory, it causes violent behavior in lab

animals. Additionally, other forms of epilepsy do not cause abnormalities in behavior, except during seizure activity. Temporal lobe epilepsy is linked with a wide range of antisocial behavior, including anger, paranoia, and aggression. It is also interesting to note that this form of epilepsy produces extremely unusual brain waves. These waves have been found in only 10 to 15 percent of the general population, but over 79 percent of known serial killers test positive for these waves (Taylor 28–33).

The look at biological factors that control human behavior is by no means limited to brain waves or other brain abnormalities. Much work is also being done with neurotransmitters, levels of testosterone, and patterns of trace minerals. While none of these studies is conclusive, they all show a high correlation between antisocial behavior and chemical interactions within the body (Taylor 63–69). 9

One of the most common traits that all researchers have noted among serial killers is heavy use of alcohol. Whether this correlation is brought about by external factors or whether alcohol is an actual stimulus that causes certain behavior is still unclear, but the idea deserves consideration. Lunde found that the majority of those who commit murder had been drinking beforehand and commonly had a urine alcohol level of between .20 and .29, nearly twice the legal level of intoxication (31–32). Additionally, 70 percent of the families that reared serial killers had verifiable records of alcohol abuse (Ressler, Burgess, and Douglas 17). Jeffrey Dahmer had been arrested in 1981 on charges of drunkenness, and before his release from prison on sexual assault charges, his father had written a heartbreaking letter pleading that Jeffrey be forced to undergo treatment for alcoholism—a plea that, if heeded, might have changed the course of future events (Davis 70, 103). Whether alcoholism is a learned behavior or an inherited predisposition is still hotly debated, but a 1979 report issued by Harvard Medical School stated that "[a]lcoholism in the biological parent appears to be a more reliable predictor of alcoholism in the children than any other environmental factor examined" (qtd. in Taylor 117). While alcohol was once thought to alleviate anxiety and depression, we now know that it can aggravate and intensify such moods; for the serial killers this may lead to irrational feelings of powerlessness that are brought under control only when the killer proves he has the ultimate power to control life and death (Taylor 110). 10

"Man's inhumanity to man" began when Cain killed Abel, but this legacy has grown to frightening proportions, as evidenced by the 11 vast number of books that line the shelves of bookstores today—row after row of titles dealing with death, anger, and blood. We may never know what causes a serial killer to exact his revenge on an unsuspecting society, but we need to continue to probe the interior of the human brain to discover the delicate balance of chemicals that controls behavior; we need to be able to fix what goes wrong. We must also work harder to protect our children. Their cries must not go unheard; their pain must not become so intense that it demands bloody revenge. As today becomes tomorrow, we must remember the words of Ted Bundy, one of the most ruthless serial killers of our time: "Most serial killers are people who kill for the pure pleasure of killing and cannot be rehabilitated. Some of the killers themselves would even say so" (qtd. in Holmes and DeBurger 150).

## WORKS CITED

Biondi, Ray, and Walt Hecox. *The Dracula Killer.* New York: Simon, 1992.

Davis, Ron. *The Milwaukee Murders.* New York: St. Martin's, 1991.

Holmes, Ronald M., and James DeBurger. *Serial Murder.* Newbury Park: Sage, 1988.

Lunde, Donald T. *Murder and Madness.* San Francisco: San Francisco Book, 1976.

Markman, Ronald, and Dominick Bosco. *Alone with the Devil.* New York: Doubleday, 1989.

Ressler, Robert K., Ann W. Burgess, and John E. Douglas. *Sexual Homicide—Patterns and Motives.* Lexington: Heath, 1988.

Samenow, Stanton E. *Inside the Criminal Mind.* New York: Times, 1984.

Taylor, Lawrence. *Born to Crime.* Westport: Greenwood, 1984.

# *The Rise in Reported Incidents of Workplace Sexual Harassment*

**Sarah West**

*University of Houston*
*Houston, Texas*

To those students who recently graduated from high school, it may sound like the Dark Ages, but it wasn't: until 1964, an employee who refused to give in to his or her employer's sexual advances could be fired—legally. An employee being constantly humiliated by a co-worker could be forced to either deal with the lewd comments, the stares, and the touching or just quit his or her job. It is truly strange to think that sexual harassment was perfectly legal in the United States until Congress passed the Civil Rights Act of 1964. 1

But even after 1964, sexual harassment still persisted. It was not widely known exactly what sexual harassment was or that federal laws against it existed. Often when an employee was sexually harassed on the job, he or she felt too alienated and humiliated to speak out against it (Martell and Sullivan 6). During the 1970s and 1980s, however, sexual harassment victims began coming forward to challenge their harassers. Then suddenly in the 1990s, the number of sexual harassment complaints and lawsuits sharply rose. According to a 1994 survey conducted by the Society for Human Resource Management, the percentage of human resource professionals who have reported that their departments handled at least one sexual harassment complaint rose from 35 percent in 1991 to 65 percent in 1994 (*Sexual*). Why did this large increase occur in such a short amount of time? Possible answers to this question surely would include growing awareness of the nature of workplace sexual harassment, government action, efforts of companies to establish anti-harassment policies and encourage harassed employees to come forward, and prominence given by the media to many cases of workplace harassment. 2

One significant cause of the rise in reported incidents of sexual harassment was most likely the increased awareness of what constitutes sexual harassment. There are two distinct types of sexual 3 harassment, and although their formal names may be unfamiliar, the situations they describe will most certainly ring a bell. *Hostile environment* sexual harassment occurs when a supervisor or coworker gives the victim "unwelcome sexual attention" that "interferes with (his or her) ability to work or creates an intimidating or offensive atmosphere" (Stanko and Werner 15). *Quid pro quo* sexual harassment occurs when "a workplace superior demands some degree of sexual favor" and either threatens to or does retaliate in a way that "has a tangible effect on the working conditions of the harassment victim" if he or she refuses to comply (Stanko and Werner 15).

A fundamental cause of the rise in reports of workplace harassment was government action in 1964 and again in 1991. After the passage of the Civil Rights Act of 1991, which allowed, among other things, larger damage awards for sexually harassed employees, many more employees began coming forward with complaints. They realized that sexual harassment was not legal and they could do something about it. Suddenly, it became possible for a company to lose millions in a single sexual harassment case. For example, Rena Weeks, a legal secretary in San Francisco, sued the law firm of Baker & McKenzie for $3.5 million after an employee, Martin Greenstein, "dumped candy down the breast pocket of her blouse, groped her, pressed her from behind and pulled her arms back 'to see which one (breast) is bigger'" ("Workplace"). The jury awarded Weeks $7.1 million in punitive damages, twice what she sought in her lawsuit ("Workplace"). In addition, research revealed that the mere existence of sexual harassment in a company could lead to "hidden costs" such as absenteeism, lower productivity, and loss of valuable employees (Stanko and Werner 16). 4

Concerned about these costs, most companies decided to develop and publicize sexual harassment policies, making every employee aware of the problem and more likely to come forward as early as possible so that employers have a chance to remedy the situation before it gets out of hand. Prior to 1991, sexual harassment victims were often asked by their employers simply to remain silent (Martell and Sullivan 8). These new policies and procedures, along with training sessions, made it much more likely that employees would report incidents of sexual harassment. And we should not be surprised that the Internet has provided independent information to employees about dealing with workplace sexual harassment ("Handling"; "Sexual"). 5

The media have also contributed to the rise of reports of workplace sexual harassment by giving great attention to a few prominent 6 cases. In 1991, Supreme Court Justice Clarence Thomas in Senate hearings on his nomination had to defend himself from sexual harassment charges by his former colleague Anita Hill. Later that same year, male U.S. navy officers were accused of sexually harassing female navy officers at the infamous Tailhook Convention, a yearly gathering of navy aviators (Nelton 24). During the late 1990s, Paula Jones's sexual harassment charges against President Clinton dominated the national news on many days. Jones was an Arkansas state employee at the time she said Clinton, who was then governor, harassed her. These three highly publicized cases made sexual harassment a much-discussed issue that sparked debate and encouraged victims to come forward.

Not everyone believes that there has been an increase in reports 7
of workplace harassment. One journalist, writing in 1995, has argued that the rise in reported sexual harassment complaints is actually a sort of illusion caused by insufficient research, since "research on this topic has only been undertaken since the 1970s" (Burke 23). This journalist seems to be the one suffering from an illusion or an unwillingness to read the research. Clearly, as the Society for Human Resource Management shows, there was a sharp rise in complaints between 1991, when the Civil Rights Act was passed, and the mid-1990s. Has there been a steady increase in reported incidents since 1964? I do not know and am not focusing on that period. The noticeable increase in complaints from 1991 to 1994—from 35 percent to 65 percent (*Sexual*)—is enough to establish a trend.

It has also been suggested that the trend is the result of a 8
greater percentage of women in the workplace (Martell and Sullivan 5). This may be a sufficient argument since women report sexual harassment in a significantly greater number of cases than men do (men report roughly one-tenth of what women report). It has been noted, however, that there has been a rise in sexual harassment complaints reported by male victims as well recently. According to the Equal Employment Opportunity Commission, the number of sexual harassment complaints filed annually by men more than doubled from 1989 to 1993 (Corey). Sexual harassment is by no means a new occurrence. It has most likely existed since workplace environments have existed. The increased number of women in the workplace today has likely increased the percentage of women workers being sexually harassed, but it is also very plausible that the rise in reported incidents of sexual harassment is because of increased

awareness of sexual harassment and the steps that one can legally take to stop it.

It has taken thirty years, but American society seems to be making significant progress in bringing a halt to a serious problem. *Sexual harassment,* a phrase that was unfamiliar to most of us only a few years ago, is now mentioned almost daily on television and in newspapers. We can only hope that the problem will end if we continue to hear about, read about, and, most important, talk about sexual harassment and its negative consequences as we educate each other about sexual harassment. Then, perhaps someday, sexual harassment can be stopped altogether. 9

## WORKS CITED

Burke, Ronald J. "Incidence and Consequences of Sexual Harassment in a Professional Services Firm." *Employee Counseling Today* Feb. 1995: 23–29.

Corey, Mary. "On-the-Job Sexism Isn't Just a Man's Sin Anymore." *Houston Chronicle* 30 Aug. 1993: D1.

"Handling Sexual Harassment Complaints." *Employer and Employee* 1997. 8 Jan. 1998 <http://www.employer-employee.com/sexhar1.html>.

Martell, Kathryn, and George Sullivan. "Strategies for Managers to Recognize and Remedy Sexual Harassment." *Industrial Management* May/June 1994: 5–8.

Nelton, Sharon. "Sexual Harassment: Reducing the Risks." *Nation's Business* Mar. 1995: 24–26.

"Sexual Harassment FAQ." *Employment: Workplace Rights and Responsibilities* 1998. 8 Jan. 1998 <http://www.nolo.com/ChunkEMP/emp7.html>.

*Sexual Harassment Remains a Workplace Problem, but Most Employers Have Policies in Place, SHRM Survey Finds.* Alexandria: Society for Human Resource Management, 26 June 1994: 1.

Stanko, Brian B., and Charles A. Werner. "Sexual Harassment: What Is It? How to Prevent It." *National Public Accountant* June 1995: 14–16.

"Workplace Bias Suits." *USA Today* 30 Nov. 1994: B2.

# *Pharmaceutical Advertising*

**Krista Gonnerman**

*Rose-Hulman Institute of Technology*
*Terre Haute, Indiana*

Turn on the television, wait for the commercial breaks, and you are guaranteed to see them: direct-to-consumer (DTC) pharmaceutical advertisements. In fact, "Americans now see an average of nine prescription ads per day on televison" (McLean). Allegra, an allergy medication; Celebrex, a medication for arthritis pain; Claritin, another allergy medication; Detral, a pill to help control overactive bladder; Lamisil, a drug to combat toenail fungus; Lipitor, a medication used to lower cholesterol; Nexium, an acid reflux medication; Procrit, a medication meant to increase red blood cell production; Viagra, a medication for impotence; Vioxx, an anti-inflammatory medication; Zocor, another medication meant to lower cholesterol; Zoloft, an antidepressant—the list of drugs currently promoted on television seems endless and overwhelming. Flashy, celebrity endorsed, emotionally appealing, with snappy tag lines and occasionally catchy tunes, these thirty-second sound bites typically show healthy people enjoying life. According to one source, the pharmaceutical industry "has tripled drug advertising since 1996 to nearly $2.5 billion a year. . . . Of the print and broadcast ads, 60% were for just 20 medications" ("NJBIZ"); industry spending is "up 28% from 1999 and 40 times the $55 million spent on mass media ads in 1991" (McLean); in 1998 alone, the drug companies spent more than $500 million solely on television advertising (West). 1

The most significant and largely encompassing cause behind this veritable explosion of pharmaceutical advertisements on television occurred in 1997 when the Federal Drug Administration (FDA) relaxed the regulations overseeing pharmaceutical advertising on television. Prior to 1997, the FDA regulations addressing prescription drug advertisements were so strict that few manufacturers bothered to promote their drugs in the media. Those drug manufacturers 2 who sought to advertise on television were restricted to broadcasting "a drug's name without stating its purpose. Or stating a drug's purpose without saying its name. Or stating a drugs [sic] name and medical purpose only if the patient insert was scrolled on the screen" (West). But in 1996 the pharmaceutical industry filed a freedom of speech challenge and won, and in August 1997 the FDA's Division of Drug Marketing and Communications issued the revised regulations that are still in effect today. Currently, "[d]rug companies can now tell viewers . . . what their drug is used for without reciting or scrolling the entire Patient Insert; a major statement of serious side effects and a phone number or other route of obtaining the rest of the information" is now all that is required of the commercial (West). No longer hampered by restrictions, the pharmaceutical industry began in 1997 and has continued to focus its advertising budget on television: "The National Institute for Health Care Management in Washington reports that $1.8 billion was spent on d-t-c pharmaceutical advertising last year [1999], with $1.1 billion on TV" (Liebeskind).

A second, but debatable, cause may originate in patients becoming more proactive in their own healthcare. Both Carol Lewis, writing in *FDA Consumer,* and Dr. Sidney Wolfe, writing in the *New England Journal of Medicine*, note that beginning in the mid-1980s there was an increase in the number of individuals (1) seeking more medical information than they were being given by their doctors and (2) making medical decisions affecting their own healthcare. Lewis and Wolfe suggest that based on the pharmaceutical industry's awareness of this ground swell, the industry may have begun producing ads aimed at such consumers. Yet beyond this anecdotal, undocumented evidence by Lewis and Wolfe, there is little to support the suggestion that greater patient involvement led to the dramatic increase in pharmaceutical advertisements on television. 3

Other causes for the proliferation of pharmaceutical advertisements have been suggested, but these ideas lack merit. For example, it has been suggested that since many individuals do not want to make the necessary lifestyle changes, such as exercising and eating healthier, changes that would result in true health benefits, the pharmaceutical industry began running commercials, in part, to encourage individuals to seek out their doctors as a first step toward a healthier life. But the pharmaceutical industry is a for-profit industry, and its DTC commercials look to market products for the primary purpose of enhancing pharmaceutical companies' bottom-lines, not 4 to encourage consumers to embrace healthier lifestyles that will lead to their—potentially—not needing medications.

5 In a similar vein, "The Coalition for Healthcare Communication, a group of advertising agencies and medical publications dependent on drug advertising, said that an analysis of leading published consumer surveys provides strong evidence that [DTC] advertising of prescription drugs is a valued source of health care information" ("Drug Industry"). In other words, the pharmaceutical industry began running the ads as a way of providing information-hungry patients with reliable knowledge. But as Maryann Napoli sarcastically notes, "Anyone trying to sell you something isn't going to give you the most balanced picture of the product's effectiveness and risks." Or as Dr. Wolfe writes, "The education of patients . . . is too important to be left to the pharmaceutical industry, with its pseudo educational campaigns designed, first and foremost, to promote drugs."

6 The 1997 FDA regulatory revisions on media advertisements provided the pharmaceutical industry the opportunity to inundate television with its products. But as consumers we should not blindly accept what we see in the industry's thirty-second sound bites. While we can use the information conveyed in the commercials to help us make more informed decisions about our own healthcare or use the information in consultation with our physicians, we must never forget that the commercials are meant to sell products, and if those products improve our health, it is merely a consequence of the industry's primary intention.

## WORKS CITED

"Drug Industry Study Finds Direct-to-Consumer Ads Help Customers." *Health Care Strategic Management* July 2001: 10.

Liebeskind, Ken. "Targeted Ads for New Drugs a Shot in the Arm." *Editor & Publisher* Nov. 2000: 33.

Lewis, Carol. "The Impact of Direct-to-Consumer Advertising." *FDA Consumer* Mar/Apr. 2003: 9. *MasterFILE Premier*. EBSCO. Rose-Hulman Inst. of Tech. Lib. 20 May 2003 <http://epnet.com>.

McLean, Candis. "The Real Drug Pushers." *Report/Newsmagazine* 19 Mar. 2001: 38–42. *MasterFILE Premier*. EBSCO. Rose-Hulman Inst. of Tech. Lib. 20 May 2003 <http://epnet.com>.

Napoli, Maryann. "Those Omnipresent Prescription Drug Ads: What to Look Out For." *Healthfacts* June 2001: 3.

"NJBIZ." *Business News New Jersey* 25 Feb. 2002: 3–5. *MasterFILE Premier.* EBSCO. Rose-Hulman Inst. of Tech. Lib. 20 May 2003 <http://epnet.com>.

West, Diane. "DTC Ponders the Twilight Zone of TV Advertising." *Pharmaceutical Executive* May 1999: A4–A8. *MasterFILE Premier.* EBSCO. Rose-Hulman Inst. of Tech. Lib. 20 May 2003 <http://epnet.com>.

Wolfe, Sidney M. "Direct-to-Consumer Advertising—Education or Emotion Promotion?" *New England Journal of Medicine* 346.7 (2002): 524–26. *MasterFILE Premier.* EBSCO. Rose-Hulman Inst. of Tech. Lib. 20 May 2003 <http://epnet.com>.

# 10 *Interpreting Stories*

Once you learn how to analyze stories, interpreting them can lead you to insights, both literary and personal. Both Sarah Hawkins and Margaret Tate present strong interpretations. The structure of Hawkins's essay exploring D. H. Lawrence's "In Love" reveals something of her reading strategy. She responds to words, motifs, and statements that intrigue her, interpreting them for the way they suggest and contribute to the pattern of "being in love" that forms her thesis. Her structural plan is straightforward: examine each character in turn for the mode of "being in love" that the character exemplifies.

Margaret Tate's essay on Susan Glaspell's "A Jury of Her Peers" is interesting on a number of counts. She begins with a forecasting statement at the end of the first paragraph but doesn't articulate her thesis—that "men and women vary greatly in their perception of things"—until the last paragraph. It's as if the forecasting statement sets her off and running to gather the evidence that finally "adds up" to her conclusion. It isn't just Tate's skillful literary perception and creative interpretation that make the essay succeed; it's the way she puts everything together. Instead of simply collecting examples that interest her in the text and loosely arranging them, Tate interconnects her ideas with strong supporting evidence in a tight, coherent tapestry of meaning that enriches and extends her initial insight.

# *Synopsis: D. H. Lawrence's "In Love"*

"In Love," a short story by D. H. Lawrence, opens with twenty-five-year-old Hester anxiously fretting about a weekend visit to the farm cottage of her fiancé, Joe. On this day a month before the wedding, Hester's younger sister, Henrietta, confronts her and tells her point-blank that she needs to snap out of her pout and "either put a better face on it, or . . . don't go." Although Hester does make the trip, she is never comfortable with her decision.

The crux of Hester's problem is that she and Joe had been good friends for years before she finally promised to marry him. Hester had always respected Joe as a hardworking, "decent" fellow, but now that they are to marry, she finds him changed. What she detests is the fact that, in her view, he seems to have made "the wretched mistake of falling 'in love' with her." To Hester, this notion of being in love, accentuated by all of Joe's "lovey-dovey" attempts to cuddle and snuggle and kiss, is completely idiotic and ridiculous.

After she arrives at Joe's farm cottage, Hester avoids his advances by asking him to play the piano. As he concentrates on his fingering, she slips outside into the night air and, when Joe comes looking for her, remains hidden in a tree. Alone in the dark, Hester falls into a fit of internal questioning, doubt, and upset concerning "the mess" her life seems to have become. Then suddenly, in the midst of her anxiety, who should arrive but Henrietta, claiming she is in the neighborhood on a visit to a friend down the road. Hester leaps at the chance to join Henrietta and thus escape her entrapment with Joe. When Joe hears this, however, he responds angrily, accusing the two sisters of playing a "game."

In the confrontation that follows, Hester and Joe, for the first time, speak honestly of their feelings. Hester tells Joe she detests his "making love" to her. Joe responds that she's mistaken, that he was in fact not "in love" with her but was behaving in such a manner only because he thought that "it was expected." In the conversation, Joe goes on to reveal his dilemma and his true feelings about Hester: "What are you to do," he says, "when you know a girl's rather strict, and you like her for it?"

In speaking the truth of their hearts to each other for the first time, the couple is able to reveal the depth of their feelings. They recognize that they've betrayed the intimacy of their relationship because they've acted on the basis of expectations rather than on the basis of genuine emotion. By acknowledging these facts, the couple is able to reach new understanding. Seeing Joe's honest love, Hester feels herself responding to him and, in the end, decides to stay with him. She will accept whatever he does, she says, as long as he really loves her.

# *In Love*

**Sarah Hawkins**

*University of California, San Diego*
*La Jolla, California*

1 For most people, the phrase *in love* brings many rosy pictures to mind: a young man looking into the eyes of the girl he loves, a couple walking along the beach holding hands, two people making sacrifices to be together. These stereotypes about what love is and how lovers should act can be very harmful. In his short story "In Love," D. H. Lawrence uses the three main characters to embody his theme that love is experienced in a unique way by every couple and that there isn't a normal or proper way to be in love.

2 Hester; her fiancé, Joe; and her sister, Henrietta, all approach and respond to love in different ways. Hester is unwilling to compromise what she really feels for Joe, but she is pressured by her own notions of how a young woman in her situation should feel. Joe appears to be the typical young man in love. He seems at ease with the situation, and his moves are so predictable they could have come straight from a movie script. But when he is confronted and badgered by Hester and Henrietta, he admits that he was only putting on an act and feels regret for not being honest with Hester. Henrietta is the mouthpiece for all of society's conceptions of love. She repeatedly asks Hester to be normal and secretly worries that Hester will call off the wedding. Henrietta is like a mother hen, always making sure that Hester is doing the right thing (in Henrietta's opinion, anyway).

3 Hester and Joe are, in a sense, playing a game with each other. Both are acting on what they feel is expected of them now that they are engaged, as if how they really feel about each other is unimportant. It is only when Hester and Joe finally talk honestly about their relationship that they realize they have been in love all along in their own unique way.

4 Hester, ever the practical one, becomes more and more frustrated with "Joe's love-making" (650). She feels ridiculous, as if she

is just a toy, but at the same time she feels she should respond positively to Joe, "because she believed that a nice girl would have been only too delighted to go and sit 'there'" (650). Rather than doing what she wants, enjoying a nice, comfortable relationship with Joe, Hester does what she feels she ought to. She says that she ought to like Joe's lovemaking even though she doesn't really know why. Despite her practical and independent nature, Hester is still troubled by what society would think.

Lawrence seems to be suggesting a universal theme here. If Hester, with such firm ideas about what she wants, is so troubled by what society dictates, then how much more are we, as generally less objective and more tractable people, affected by society's standards? Hester's is a dilemma everyone faces. 5

At the heart of Hester's confusion is Joe, whose personality was so different before they became engaged that Hester might not have gotten engaged if she had known how Joe would change: "Six months ago, Hester would have enjoyed it [being alone with Joe]. They were so perfectly comfortable together, he and she" (649). But by cuddling and petting, Joe has ruined the comfortable relationship that he and Hester had enjoyed. The most surprising line in the story is Hester's assertion that "[t]he very fact of his being in love with me proves that he doesn't love me" (652). Here, Hester makes a distinction between really loving someone and just putting on an act of being *in* love. Hester feels hurt that Joe would treat her as a typical girl rather than as the young woman she really is. 6

Hester is a reluctant player in the love game until the end of the story when she confronts Joe and blurts out, "I absolutely can't stand your making love to me, if that is what you call the business" (656–57). Her use of the word *business* is significant because it refers to a chore, something that has to be done. Hester regards Joe's lovemaking as if it were merely a job to be completed. When Joe apologizes, Hester sees his patient, real love for her, and she begins to have the same feelings for him again. When she says, "I don't mind what you do if you love me really" (660), Hester, by compromising, shows the nature of their love for each other. 7

Lawrence uses Joe to show a typical response to society's pressures. Joe obediently plays the role of the husband-to-be. He exhibits all the preconceived images one may have about a man about to be married. In trying to fit the expectations of others, Joe sacrifices his straightforwardness and the honesty that Hester valued so much in him. Although Joe's actions don't seem to be so bad in and of 8 themselves, in the context of his relationship with Hester they are completely out of place. His piano playing, for example, inspires Hester to remark that Joe's love games would be impossible to handle after the music he played. The music represents something that is pure and true—in contrast to the new, hypocritical Joe. Joe doesn't seem to be aware of Hester's feelings until she comes forward with them at the end of the story. The humiliation he suffers makes him silent, and he is described several times as wooden, implying stubbornness and solidness. It is out of this woodenness that a changed Joe appears. At first the word suggests his defensiveness for his bruised ego, but then as Joe begins to see Hester's point about being truly in love, his woodenness is linked to his solidness and stability, qualities that represent for Hester the old Joe. Once Joe gets his mind off the love game, the simple intimacy of their relationship is revealed to him, and he desires Hester, not in a fleeting way but in a way that one desires something that was almost lost.

Henrietta serves as the antagonist in this story because it is through her that society's opinions come clear. In almost the first line of text, Henrietta, looking at Hester, states, "If I had such a worried look on my face, when I was going down to spend the weekend with the man I was engaged to—and going to be married to in a month—well! I should either try and change my face or hide my feelings, or something" (647). With little regard for Hester's feelings, Henrietta is more concerned that Hester have the right attitude. Although Henrietta herself is not married, the fact that Hester, who is twenty-five, is soon to be married is a relief to her. Not wanting her sister to be an old maid, Henrietta does all she can to make sure the weekend runs smoothly. She acts as though Hester were her responsibility and even offers to come with Hester to take the "edge off the intimacy" (648). Being young, Henrietta hasn't really formed her own views of life or love yet. As a result, she easily believes the traditional statements society makes about love. When Hester says that she can't stand Joe's being in love with her, Henrietta keeps responding that a man is supposed to be in love with the woman he marries. She doesn't understand the real love that Joe and Hester eventually feel but only the "ought-tos" of love imposed by society. It is unclear at the end of the story if Henrietta really recognizes the new bond between Hester and Joe. 9

What society and common beliefs dictate about being in love isn't really important. In order to be happy, couples must find their own unique bond of love and not rely on others' opinions or 10 definitions. Joe and Hester come to this realization only after they are hurt and left unfulfilled as a result of the love game they play with each other. Hester knew how she really felt from the beginning, but pressure about what she *ought* to feel worried her. Joe willingly went along with the game until he realized how important their simple intimacy really was. In the end, Hester and Joe are in love not because of the games they play but because of an intimate friendship that had been growing all along.

## WORK CITED

Lawrence, D. H. "In Love." *The Complete Short Stories.* Vol. 3. New York: Penguin, 1977.

# *Synopsis: Susan Glaspell's "A Jury of Her Peers"*

Susan Glaspell's short story "A Jury of Her Peers" begins when three men and two women—Mr. Peters, the county sheriff; Mr. Henderson, the county attorney; and Mr. Hale, a farmer; along with two wives, Mrs. Peters and Mrs. Hale—begin to investigate the death of a farm neighbor, John Wright, who they believe was murdered the previous day by his wife, Mrs. Wright. Although there is no direct evidence linking her to the crime, Mrs. Wright is nevertheless jailed on suspicion of murder.

At the Wright farmhouse, the county attorney asks Mr. Hale, the man who by chance discovered the murder, to recount his experience at the farmhouse. Mr. Hale describes how he found Mrs. Wright sitting in a rocking chair as she calmly told him that Mr. Wright was upstairs dead with a rope around his neck.

As the three men search the farmhouse for evidence that might establish a motive for the crime, Mrs. Peters and Mrs. Hale sit in Mrs. Wright's kitchen. With attentive eyes, they keenly observe domestic details that begin to reveal a pattern of meaning that the men overlook. As they continue to look around, the details begin to speak volumes about the emotional lives and marital relationship of Mr. and Mrs. Wright. Mrs. Peters and Mrs. Hale notice the uncharacteristic dirty pans and towels in the kitchen, neither of which fit Mrs. Wright's character as a careful housekeeper. They note a half-full bag of sugar that, again, is uncharacteristic, suggesting an interrupted task. They find a single square on Mrs. Wright's quilt that is raggedly sewn—just one, amidst a field of perfectly sewn pieces—which suggests the seamstress had to be out of sorts with herself.

As these domestic details add up, they gain significance for the women while the men scoff and dismiss their concerns as simplistic and typical of women. Finally, when the women discover a birdcage with its door broken and then—at the bottom of the sewing basket—a dead canary wrapped in silk, its neck wrung, they realize they have stumbled upon the motive for the murder. Bound up in the details of violence and dishonor—the husband killed the wife's canary—Mrs. Peters and Mrs. Hale discover the joyless horror Mrs. Wright endured in her marriage to her hard, uncaring husband. They realize John Wright was the man who killed not only a canary but also the spirit of his wife, a woman who had been a beautiful singer—a songbird—in her youth. Mrs. Peters and Mrs. Hale draw on personal experiences to empathize with Mrs. Wright. Mrs. Peters recalls the raging desire to hurt the boy who killed her kitten when she was a girl, and Mrs. Hale recalls the stillness she felt when her first baby died, likening it to the stillness that Mrs. Wright must have endured in her loveless marriage.

In the end, Mrs. Peters's and Mrs. Hale's empathy for Mrs. Wright is so deep that when the men return to collect them to leave, the women look at each other quickly and Mrs. Hale stuffs the dead bird into her coat pocket. Without concrete evidence to establish a motive for murder, they know a jury will not convict the woman. Mrs. Peters and Mrs. Hale act as Mrs. Wright's first jury—a true jury of her peers, relying on experience, intuition, and empathy rather than legal reasoning to find justice in their world.

# *Irony and Intuition in "A Jury of Her Peers"*

**Margaret Tate**

*DeKalb College*
*Decatur, Georgia*

Though men and women are now recognized as generally equal in talent and intelligence, when Susan Glaspell wrote "A Jury of Her Peers" in 1917, it was not so. In this turn-of-the-century, rural midwestern setting, women were often barely educated and possessed virtually no political or economic power. And, being considered the weaker sex, there was not much they could do about it. Relegated to home and hearth, women found themselves at the mercy of the more powerful men in their lives. Ironically, it is just this type of powerless existence, perhaps, that over the ages developed into a power with which women could baffle and frustrate their male counterparts: a sixth sense — an inborn trait commonly known as women's intuition. In Glaspell's story, ironic situations contrast male and female intuition, illustrating that Minnie Wright is more fairly judged by women than by men. 1

"A Jury of Her Peers" first uses irony to illustrate the contrast between male and female intuition when the men go to the farmhouse looking for clues to the murder of John Wright, but it is the women who find them. In the Wright household, the men are searching for something out of the ordinary, an obvious indication that Minnie has been enraged or provoked into killing her husband. Their intuition does not tell them that their wives, because they are women, can help them gain insight into what has occurred between John and his wife. They bring Mrs. Hale and Mrs. Peters along merely to tend to the practical matters, considering them needlessly preoccupied with trivial things and even too unsophisticated to make a contribution to the investigation, as illustrated by Mr. Hale's derisive question, "Would the women know a clue if they did come upon it?" (289). 2

Ironically, while the men are looking actively for the smoking gun, the women are confronted with subtler clues in spite of themselves and even try to hide from each other what they intuitively 3 know. But they do not fool each other for long, as Glaspell describes: "Their eyes met—something flashed to life, passed between them; then, as if with an effort, they seemed to pull away from each other" (295). However, they cannot pull away, for they are bound by a power they do not even comprehend: "We all go through the same things—it's all just a different kind of the same thing! . . . why do you and I *understand*? Why do we *know*—what we know this minute?" (303). They do not realize that it is intuition they share, that causes them to "[see] into things, [to see] through a thing to something else . . ." (294). Though sympathetic to Minnie Wright, the women cannot deny the damning clues that lead them to the inescapable conclusion of her guilt.

If it is ironic that the women find the clues, it is even more ironic that they find them in the mundane household items to which the men attribute so little significance. "Nothing here but kitchen things," the men mistakenly think (287). Because of their weak intuition, they do not see the household as indicative of John's and Minnie's characters. They do not see beyond the cheerless home to John Wright's grim nature, nor do the dilapidated furnishings provide them with a clue to his penurious habits. Minnie's depression and agitation are not apparent to them in the dismal, half-cleaned kitchen; instead, they consider Minnie an inept, lazy housekeeper. Oddly, for all their "snoopin' round and criticizin'" (290), the three gentlemen literally do not have a clue. 4

The women, on the other hand, "used to worrying over trifles" (287), do attach importance to the "everyday things" (299), and looking around the cheerless kitchen, they see many examples of the miserably hard existence of Minnie Wright. Knowing the pride a woman takes in her home, they see Minnie's kitchen not as dirty, but as half-cleaned, and the significance of this is not lost on them. And, upon discovering the erratic quilt stitching, they are alarmed. Also, they cannot dismiss the broken birdcage as just a broken birdcage. They instinctively know, as the men do not, that Minnie desperately needed a lively creature to brighten up such a loveless home. Upon finding these clues, ironically hidden in everyday objects, the women piece them together with a thread of intuition and create a blanket of guilt that covers the hapless Minnie Wright. 5

Though there is irony in the fact that the women, not the men, find the clues, and irony in the fact that they are found in everyday household things, most ironic is the fact that John Wright meets the same fate he has inflicted on the poor bird, illustrating that he is 6 perhaps the least intuitive of all the men in the story. John Wright never sees beyond his own needs to the needs of his wife. He does not understand her need for a pretty creature to fill the void created by her lonely, childless existence. Not content to kill just Minnie's personality ("[s]he was [once] kind of like a bird herself. Real sweet and pretty" [299]), he kills her canary, leaving her with the deafening silence of the lonesome prairie. Minnie has endured many years of misery at the hands of John Wright, but he pushes her too far when he kills the bird. Then, ironically, he gets the "peace and quiet" (283) he values over her happiness.

John Wright lacks the intuition to understand his wife's love of 7
her bird, but the two women do not. They understand that she needed the bird to fill the still air with song and lessen her loneliness. After discovering the dead bird, they do not blame her for killing John. The dead bird reminds Mrs. Peters of a traumatic episode from her childhood:

> "When I was a girl," said Mrs. Peters, under her breath, "my kitten—there was a boy took a hatchet, and before my eyes—before I could get there. . . . If they hadn't held me back, I would have . . . hurt him." (301–02)

The women see the reason for Minnie's murderous impulse, but they know that the men lack the insight to ever fully understand her situation or her motivation; therefore, in hiding the bird, by their silence, they acquit Minnie Wright.

Through the ironic situations in "A Jury of Her Peers," Glaspell 8
clearly illustrates a world in which men and women vary greatly in their perception of things. She shows men as often superficial in the way they perceive the world, lacking the depth of intuition that women use as a means of self-preservation to see themselves and the world more clearly. Without the heightened perspective on life that this knowledge of human nature gives them, women might not stand a chance. Against the power and domination of men, they often find themselves as defenseless and vulnerable as Minnie's poor bird.

## WORK CITED

Glaspell, Susan. "A Jury of Her Peers." *Lifted Masks and Other Works.* Ed. Eric S. Rabkin. Ann Arbor: U of Michigan P, 1993.

# *A Note on the Copyediting*

We all know that the work of professional writers rarely appears in print without first being edited. But what about student writing—especially essays that are presented *as models* of student writing? Do these get edited too?

This is not as clear-cut an issue as it may first appear. While it's easy to draw an analogy with professional writing and simply declare that "all published writing gets edited," there are some important differences between student and professional writing. For one thing, student writing is presented *as student writing*. That is, it's offered to the reader as an example of the kind of writing students can and do produce in a writing class. And since most students don't have the benefit of a professional editor to read their work before it's graded, their work may not be as polished as the models they see in textbooks.

For another, students whose work appears in publications like this one rarely have the opportunity to participate in the editorial process. Publication schedules being what they are, text authors and editors often don't know exactly what they want in terms of example essays until late in the process, and by then they may be so immersed in their own revising that it's difficult, if not impossible, to supervise twenty-five or more student writers as well.

For these reasons, student writers are usually simply asked to sign a statement, transferring to the publisher all rights to their essays, subject to final editing, and don't see their work again until it appears in print. That makes the situation somewhat problematic.

But publishing student essays without editing is equally problematic. Every composition teacher knows that even the best papers, the A+ essays, aren't perfect. But readers of published prose, accustomed to the conventions of edited American English, aren't always so generous. The shift in tense that may be seen as a simple lapse in a student narrative becomes a major distraction in a published piece. Rather than preserve that tense shift in the interest of "absolute fidelity" to the student's work, it is more in keeping with the spirit and purpose of the enterprise to edit the passage. After all, the rest of the evidence indicates that the student is a strong writer and that he or she would likely accede to the change if it were called to his or her attention.

In this respect, editing student essays should be seen not as a violation of the student's work but as a courtesy to the writer. True, some essays require more editing than others—perhaps because the student did not have as much opportunity to revise—but none in this collection has been altered significantly. In fact, every attempt has been made to respect the student's choices.

To give you an inside look at the editing process, we reproduce here the originally submitted version of Erick Young's essay, "Only She," along with the Bedford/St. Martin's editor's markings. It might be interesting to compare this early version with the final edited version printed on pages 33–37. What changes were made, and why? Were all of them necessary? If you were the writer, how would you react to these changes?

Finally, if you are a writer whose work has undergone editorial revision—perhaps as a result of peer critique—you might think about how the process felt to you. Did you appreciate your editor's work? Resent it? What did you learn from it? If you're like most of us, you probably realized that it's natural to resist, but necessary to accept, criticism. In other words, you learned to think of yourself as a writer.

# *Sample Copyediting*

Erick Young

Person Essay

Rewrite

Only She

Those eyes. No no, deep, dark brown. Hardly a wrinkle around them. Soft, smooth ~~looking~~ skin. And those eyebrows. Neither thick nor thin; just bold—two curved punctuation ~~marks gracing~~ her facial expressions with a certain ~~extra accent~~. Surprise, amusement—up would shoot one of the brows, the right one I believe, just slightly, accompanied by a mischievous little smirk ~~that would curl onto her lips~~. Anger, irritation—up and inward shot both brows, tightly pressed, followed by a sharp "What d'ya want? Don't bother me!" She never really meant it though; ~~she~~ it was just saying "hello." Even though she wore glasses she could still see all, with or without them. Her deep, dark brown eyes were no ordinary ~~little masses of flesh and tissue~~ eyes; no, within those deep wells rested a pair of magic orbs, two miniature crystal balls that could peer into your mind and read all your little thoughts. Some thought she had psychic powers. She knew what you were thinking, or at least ~~so many times,~~ she ~~knew~~ always seemed to know what I was thinking; ~~all of~~ even my most complex, inexplicable thoughts. And that was all that seemed to matter at the time. Only she, only Sonia Koujakian, ~~only~~ Mrs. K.

I do not recall the first time I noticed her at school, but Mrs. K was not one to blend into ~~the~~ a crowd. ~~for very long.~~ Briskly walking across ~~our~~ the school's rotunda, I would see her, tall and lean, wearing a skirt and a mauve-colored raincoat, holding a stuffed beige handbag in one hand, and a bright red coffee pot in the other. She seemed so confident, always looking straight ahead ~~rather than down~~ as she walked about ~~the~~ school. Perhaps it was her hair that first caught my eye. It was short, ~~almost spiked, with its~~ a mix of light brown and gray ~~hairs~~ combed slightly up — almost spiked. Not the typical sort of hairstyle for an English teacher at our school. It set her apart ~~though~~ and made her look dynamic. Already I knew that she was somebody special.

The ~~beckon to take the Preliminary Scholastic Aptitude Test~~ PSAT brought ~~us together briefly~~ her into my life for the first time, in my sophomore year. ~~allowing me to get a small taste of Mrs. K's personality~~ Even though she was the senior English teacher, she ~~made an open~~ offered to coach any undaunted sophomores or juniors after school for the nefarious "SAT jr." Trying to be the savvy student, I joined ~~two other friends and accepted her offer. Only~~ a small group ~~of us~~ who gathered in her cove after school ~~the following afternoons and~~ to practiced vocabulary drills and sentence completions. Mrs. K would scold us on the finer points of grammar ~~when~~ as we reviewed our errors ~~throwing at~~ giving us her "Come on, get with the production" ~~expression.~~ look. Not the typical reaction from a ~~person one hardly knew; all the little formalities I had come to expect in a teacher student relationships had been thrown out the window with Mrs. K.~~ teacher; she treated us like peers, and would say to us what ever was on her mind without ~~any~~ pretenses, ~~niceties,~~ pleasantry, or euphemisms. We could do the same, if we had the ~~stomach~~ guts to try. Her casual disposition made me feel both relaxed and nervous; ~~I did not know~~ none of us knew how to act around her, whether to joke and tease her, or respect and honor her. ~~Most of my friends felt the same way.~~ We all ~~felt~~ agreed, however, that she ~~simply~~ was ~~down-to-Earth,~~ as down-to-earth as they come. ~~friends, teachers, or anyone. Soon, the prep sessions were over and it would not be until~~ Two years later, as an older and wiser senior, ~~that~~ I would get ~~the~~ a full ~~taste~~ dose of Mrs. K's personality.

My first day in Mrs. K's class left much to be desired. I entered to find most of my classmates just ~~sat around waiting,~~

~~talking,~~ laughing and joking. The first-day-of-school jitters had become passé, and ~~a certain~~ the smugness ~~automatically arising from the passage of four years and the arrival of~~ that comes with Seniordom dominated the room. It was ~~amongst~~ a convention of Alfred E. Neumans, and the nonchalant air of "What Me Worry?" ~~wafted in~~ filled the classroom. Some ~~of my classmates,~~ students, however, sat very quitely. ~~Some~~ These were ~~very~~ the wise ones; they'd ~~some had~~ heard about Mrs. K ~~before.~~ Academic ~~hardships~~ tensions hovered like ~~an~~ the inevitable black storm cloud above Room 5C3. There was a small fear of the unknown and the unexpected nudging about in my stomach as I sat at the far end of the center table. Strange how this was the only classroom in the entire building to have six huge wooden tables instead of forty individual little desks; someone must have wanted it that way. For once I was not too anxious to ~~be too close to the~~ sit up front. ~~Soon~~ Suddenly the chattering ~~atmosphere~~ diminished ~~into nothingness.~~ Mrs. K was coming.

In she ambled, with her stuffed ~~beige~~ handbag and bright red coffee pot, wearing a skirt and ~~her~~ the mauve raincoat; ~~it~~ she was just as I had ~~imagined.~~ remembered. She scanned the room, and up went her right eyebrow. A most peculiar "I-know-what-you-are-up-to" smirk was our first greeting. Now I was nervous.

"All right, ladies and gentlemen, I want to see if

you belong in my class," she began ~~in a soft but earnest voice.~~ "Take out a pen and lots of paper." Pause. "Now don't get too worried over this, since you are all geniuses anyway. You know, if you've got it you've got it, if you don't. . ." ~~Her shoulders~~ shrugged. Pause. "Some of you know you don't really belong in here" she chided ~~as she~~ pointed her finger, "and it's time you stopped getting put in Honors English just because ~~you have a little star by your name in the role book, meanin~~ you passed some little test ~~back~~ in second grade. Well now we're going to see what you can do" ~~she said matter-of-factly, arms akimbo, right brow up.~~ "Okay now, stop and think for a moment, and get those ~~wonderful~~ creative juices going. I want you to write me a paper telling me the origin of the English language. You can be as creative as you want. Make up something if you have to two cavemen grunting ~~to~~ each other, I don't care. You have until the end of the period. Go."

It was not the most encouraging welcome. For a moment the whole class just sort of slumped in their seats suddenly ~~phazed and drained~~ of all vitality and hopes of a relaxed senior year. Blank faces abounded Mine ~~was one of them.~~ I had no idea what to write. The origin of the English language? Being "creative" seemed too risky. What ever happened to the good ol' five paragraph essay with specific examples? Well I didn't have any specific examples anyway. I remember staring at a sheet of white paper, then scrawling down some incoherent mumbo-jumbo. I wanted to impress her, too much. I choked, and was doomed to a dismal dungeon of drudgery. I blew it with Mrs. K. "It was nice knowing you," I signed as I handed in my paper. What a first day.

That first day of class would not be my last with Mrs. K fortunately. A poor performance on the first pressure writing was not a notice of termination but rather an early warning of possible eviction. The class size shrunk the following days as some students ran for their academic lives. I was not prepared to leave. I knew Mrs. K's class would be an arduous English journey but I could never let myself miss it. It would be a journey well worth taking.

As the weeks continued, tidbits of Mrs. K's colorful past and philosophy about life would somehow always creep into our lectures and class discussions. We found out she had served as a volunteer nurse in a Japan-based combat hospital and had "seen it all even grown men cry." During the 60s a wider Mrs. K could be seen cruising the streets of San Francisco atop motorcycle, decked out in long spiked boots and short spiked hair. She later traded in her motorcycle and boots for a Fiat and white Reeboks. ~~though,~~ And there was a running joke about her age. Mrs. K could not be much less ~~younger~~ than forty-five, ~~her mid-forties.~~ but just as Jack Benny was forever thirty-nine ~~39~~, she was forever twenty-eight ~~28~~. One of her T-shirts said so. Twenty-eight was a good year, ~~for her~~ she would tell us, but she never explained quite why.

I would come to deeply trust and respect this ~~seemingly~~ eccentric lady. ~~while the school year progressed.~~ I guess I have Oedipus Rex to thank for our first out-of-class ~~close~~ meeting. We had to compose an extensive essay on the Oedipus trilogy, on which much of our semester grade would be based. Foolishly, I chose to write on the most ~~difficult~~ abstract topic, ~~concerning~~ predestination and divine justice. I toiled for days, torturing ~~inflicting upon~~ myself ~~a sort deranged mental torture~~ trying to come up with some ~~to~~ definitive conclusion~~es~~. Finally, I realized my struggle was merely carrying my mind farther and farther adrift in a sea of confusion. I needed someone to rescue me; I needed Mrs. K.

We arranged to meet in the Faculty Commons, a small, smoky room of teachers with ~~their~~ red pens at work and administrators shooting the breeze over lunch. I crept inside with notes in hand and took a seat. ~~amongst the haze.~~ She soon arrived, holding a tuna-on-wheat, a chocolate chip cookie, and the ~~a~~ red coffeepot. "I hope you don't mind if I eat while we ~~discuss~~ talk," she ~~mentioned off handly~~ said, "but if you do, I'm going to eat anyway." Smile.

We talked the whole lunch period. I felt awkward at first, actually struggling to explain why ~~I was~~ I'd been struggling ~~before~~ with the assignment. But then Mrs. K the Mentor emerged--soft spoken, introspective, wise. I opened up to her. We sat beside ~~one another~~ each other at that table, reflecting on predestination, divine justice, and life. A ray of sunshine cut through ~~my~~ clouds of confusion. Our reflections were interrupted by the lunch bell, but later we continued after school. Two days and two drafts later, I had gained more than just a deep understanding of Oedipus Rex: I had gained a friend. What was it about this woman that enabled me to reveal a different part of myself? Never before had I ~~ever~~ spoken so openly about my thoughts, ~~and~~ or about myself. Most people did not understand ~~what I was contemplating~~ my cares and thoughts. But she understood. ~~Oftentimes I did not have to explain much, her crystal balls would perform their magic.~~

I would go back to room 5C3 many afternoons later to sort my thoughts. To her I was ~~no longer Erick but~~ not Erick, Hamlet, ~~deemed~~ because of my pensive and complex nature. "Okay, Hamlet, what's on your mind?" our conversations would begin. ~~It seemed~~ Every writing assignment became an excuse to spend time after school talking and reflecting,

~~with just~~ me at the wood table ~~and~~ ~~she~~ at her stool. We digressed on everything from <u>Paradise Lost</u> to Shakespeare to ~~Robert Frost's~~ <u>The Road Not Taken</u> ~~these many afternoons~~. Sometimes other students would come ~~afterschool~~ for help on their papers, ~~but~~ I would always let them go first, so that I could be the last left. ~~Sometimes~~ I would ~~receive small lessons in life afterschool.~~ "Life's not black and white, it's a hazy gray, and you've always got to use that wonderful piece of machinery God gave you and question things because nothing is clear cut." ~~and learn more about this world~~ than just literature. I noticed my perceptions changing, as well as my writing style. More of my character entered my writing, and the Mr. Detached Impartiality persona I once favored, faded into the background. Being "creative" not longer seemed risky. She told me to put more of myself in my creations, and I listened.

~~Towards~~ the ~~close~~ of my senior year, I asked her about her favorite novel ~~during~~ one ~~last~~ afternoon. "Oh without a doubt <u>Les Misérables</u>," she replied. "But I never could find and unedited version." ~~Three days later at the end of~~ Graduation Day, ~~while~~ a sea of ~~teary eyed~~ seniors hugged one another, and red and blue ~~motorboaards~~ ~~sailed~~ through the air I searched through the crowd for Mrs. K, and handed her a small box. ~~Wrapped~~ inside with a

~~card, and a~~ long thank-you ~~on the cover,~~ note was a new copy of Les Miserables, unedited and unabridged.

I doubt that I will come across many others like Mrs. K. ~~in my life.~~ Only she would sit with me one-on-one, and review every minute detail of a draft. Only she would give up ~~many~~ an afternoon to just ~~sit down~~ shoot the breeze. Only she could I call a mentor, a confidant, and a friend. I still think of Mrs. K. Sometimes, when the pressures of college come crashing down, and the order of life seems to have run amok, I go to my room, ~~and slowly close the door and~~ shut my eyes, sit down, and talk with Mrs. K.

"Okay, Hamlet, what's on your mind. . . ."

# *Acknowledgments*

We gratefully acknowledge the following instructors who encouraged their students to submit their work for this collection or submitted the best of their students' work themselves. *Sticks and Stones* would not exist without the efforts of these instructors, and for their kindness, generosity, and participation, we are truly thankful.

Mary Amoto, Rider University
Alpha Anderson-Delap, Front Range Community College
Shelly Aubuchon, Wentworth Junior College
Susan Bailor, Front Range Community College
Tim Ballard, Riverside Community College
Lawrence Barkley, Mt. San Jacinto College, Menifee Valley
Steve Beatty, Arizona State University
Eileen Blasius, Community College of Aurora
Thomas Bonfiglio, Arizona State University
Jennie Marie Blankert, Purdue University
Kristin Brunnemer, Mt. San Jacinto College, Menifee Valley
Patricia Carlson, Rose-Hulman Institute of Technology
Susan Carlton, Bowling Green State University
Elizabeth Cranley, State University of New York at Buffalo
Michelle Croteau, Appalachian State University
Anne Dannenberg, Front Range Community College
Anne Dayton, Slippery Rock University
Dana Delker, Liberty Jr./Sr. High School
Chad Engbers, The Catholic University of America
Patricia Fels, Sacramento Country Day School
Joshua Fenton, University of California, Riverside
Z. Gimbutas, Copper Mountain College
Dorie Goldman-Rivera, Central Arizona College
Meryem Grant, Arizona State University

Gary Hawkins, University of Houston
Denise Henson, South Piedmont Community College
Richard Higgason, Blue River Community College
Valerie Holliday, Louisiana State University
Deborah Hyland, St. Louis University
Layton Isaacs, University of Houston
Jennifer Jacquot, College of St. Benedict
Rich Kempa, Western Wyoming Community College
Cordelia Koplow, Northern Kentucky University
Bonnie Landis, Anderson University
Roseanne Lyons, University School of Milwaukee
Lynda Lynner, Simpson College
Rosemary Mack, Purdue University
Catherine Maloney, North Providence High School
Sam Martinez, Mesa Community College
Ed McCorduck, State University of New York at Cortland
Rhonda McDonnell, Arizona State University
Michelle McKenzie, Arizona State University
John Melesky, Harrisburg Area Community College
Tara Miller, Wright State University
Michael Montgomery, Life University
John Mumma, Blue River Community College
Richard Nuñez, Front Range Community College
Cindy Okamura, Riverside Community College
Alison Peterson, Arizona State University
Lia Plakans, Ohio University
D. R. Ransdell, Arizona State University
Cristal Renzo, Elizabethtown College
Jeffrey Rhyne, University of California, Riverside
Jeff Ritchie, Arizona State University
Janice Ruback, North Central Michigan College
Jeff Schroetlin, Emporia State University
Gary Shapiro, Roslyn High School
Lee Smith, University of Houston
Scott Stankey, Anoka-Ramsey Community College
Joanna Tardoni, Western Wyoming Community College
Jean Timberlake, Northern Kentucky University
Sanna Towns, Metropolitan State University
Collin Wansor, Indiana University of Pennsylvania
Lisa Warmuth, Longview Community College
Sandra Weichart, Lawrence Central High School
James Wright, University of Houston

## Submitting Essays for Publication Consideration

We hope this collection is the fifth of many and that we'll be able to include more essays from more colleges and universities in the next edition. Please let us see the essays you'd like us to consider that were written using *The St. Martin's Guide to Writing.* Send them with this Essay Submission Form and the Agreement Form on the back to: English Editor—Student Essays, Bedford/St. Martin's, 33 Irving Place, 10th Floor, New York, NY 10003. You may also submit essays online at <bedfordstmartins.com/theguide>.

## Essay Submission Form

Student's name ______________________________

Instructor's name ______________________________

School ______________________________

Department ______________________________

Address ______________________________

______________________________

______________________________

Course name & number______________________________

This essay represents a writing activity that appears in chapter(s) ____________ of *The St. Martin's Guide to Writing.*

# Agreement Form

I hereby assign to Bedford/St. Martin's ("Bedford") all of my rights, title, and interest throughout the world, including without limitation, all copyrights, in and to my essay, ______________________________ (tentative title), and any notes and drafts pertaining to it (the sample essay and such materials being referred to as the "Essay").

I understand that Bedford in its discretion has the right but not the obligation to publish the Essay in any form(s) or format(s) that it may desire; that Bedford may edit, revise, condense, or otherwise alter the Essay as it deems appropriate in order to prepare the same for publication; and that Bedford is under no obligation to publish the Essay. I understand that Bedford has the right, but not the obligation, to use and to authorize the use of my name as author of the Essay in connection with any work that contains the Essay (or a portion of it).

I represent that the Essay is wholly original and was completely written by me, that publication of it will not infringe upon the rights of any third party, and that I have not granted any rights in it to any third party.

In the event Bedford determines to include any part of the Essay in *Sticks and Stones*, I will receive one free copy of that work, if any, on publication.

This Agreement constitutes the entire agreement between us concerning its subject matter and shall inure to the benefit of the successors, assignees, and licensees of Bedford.

Student's signature ______________________________

Student's name: ______________________ Date ___/___/___

*Be sure to provide us with* ***time-stable information*** *below. Please type or print clearly.*

Address(es): ______________________________

______________________________

______________________________

Phone(s) ______________________________

Email(s)______________________________

*Please indicate the chapter(s) in* Sticks and Stones *for which you would like us to consider your essay:*

| | | |
|---|---|---|
| ❑ Remembering Events | ❑ Explaining a Concept | ❑ Justifying an Evaluation |
| ❑ Remembering People | ❑ Arguing a Position | ❑ Speculating about Causes |
| ❑ Writing Profiles | ❑ Proposing a Solution | ❑ Interpreting Stories |

**You may also submit essays online at <bedfordstmartins.com/theguide>.**